LITERARY KNITS

30 PATTERNS INSPIRED BY FAVORITE BOOKS

NIKOL LOHR

WILEY

John Wiley & Sons, Inc.

Credits

Senior Editor
Roxane Cerda

Acquisitions Coordinator
Julie Hummel

Project Editor
Charlotte Kughen

Editorial Manager
Christina Stambaugh

Vice President and Publisher
Cindy Kitchel

Vice President and Executive Publisher
Kathy Nebenhaus

Interior Design
Lissa Auciello-Brogan

Cover Design
José Almaguer

Photography
Nikol Lohr, Ron Miller
(Daisy Cloche)

Dedication

*For my mom, who nurtured my love
for both books and fashion.*

Acknowledgments

Thanks most of all to my agent, Lindsay Edgecomb, who conceived the idea for this book and was generous enough to entrust it to me.

Thanks to Roxane Cerda and Cindy Kitchel, both thoughtful, engaged, and just plain fun editors; to project editors Charlotte Kughen and Carol Pogoni, who carefully whipped my manuscript into shape; and scrupulous and elegant technical editor Therese Chynoweth, who deciphered even my clumsiest instructions, smoothed out the lumps, and gave the patterns precision.

Thanks to my many friends and their children who were kind enough to model my patterns: Elise Artzer; Brian, Briza, Loretta, and Stanley Buscemi; Lucy Friedman; Rebecca Gonzales; Trish Hurless and her daughter Sadie Rose; Kyplee, Kailynn, and Treyanne Jacobsen (and their mom, Sherri); Suzanne Link and Jay Mahavier; Kristi Lohr; Rachel Kieserman; Marilyn Martinez and her daughter Ruby Martinez-Jones; Ron Miller; Charlene Osman; Lester Saucier; and Jennifer, Lucy, Sam, and Jacob Schermerhorn.

Thanks to Gilbert Garcia and Yolanda Torres for use of their cars for Sal Paradise, and to W3LL PEOPLE and makeup artist Christine Stafford for location and makeup for Emma.

Special thanks also to Ron for all the style input, and forgiving the embroidery scissors and darning needles scattered underfoot and in the bed, and for helping me keep up with the rest of my life while I was knitting and knitting and knitting.

Finally, a big thanks to all the companies that provided yarn support (that's free yarn to you and me): Spincycle Yarns, Malabrigo Yarn, Colourmart, Cascade Yarns, Louet, Valley Yarns, Blue Sky Alpacas, Lion Brand Yarn, The Wicked Stitch, and Knit Picks.

p. 111

p. 75

p. 15

p. 19

p. 96

p. 133

p. 155

p. 84

p. 61

p. 25

p. 177

p. 48

p. 103

p. 167

p. 33

Table of Contents

Preface

I can't say exactly why a love of literature and a love of knitting fit together hand-in-glove. Perhaps it's because both reading and knitting demand imagination, focus, a willing suspension of disbelief, and a bit of nerdiness. Or maybe it's because both books and knitting start with basic building blocks that can combine and recombine in any number of surprising ways.

Whatever the reason, avid knitters are very often avid readers, and I'm no exception. So when Lindsay Edgecombe (fellow knitter and literary agent) approached me about creating knitting patterns inspired by favorite literary characters, I think I actually clapped my hands and squealed with glee.

I'm not sure whether I was more thrilled to knit the designs or to re-read all my old favorites, many of which I hadn't touched since childhood. (And with the simpler patterns or with audio books, you can do both at once!)

Of course, it was nearly impossible to cull my giant master list down to a book-sized selection (and I still have a mammoth list of future designs waiting in the wings), but here I present an assortment of projects inspired by the women, men, and children from some of my favorite books. While a few items are modern-construction rewrites of antique patterns, I didn't strive for historical accuracy because I didn't want the patterns to be relegated to art pieces or historical reenactments. Instead, I tried to give a nod to the *spirit* of the character or era while still producing a very knittable, wearable, modern garment. I hope you enjoy knitting them as much as I did.

Prologue

The suggestions, techniques, and recommendations outlined provide general guidance useful for all of the patterns in the book. "Substitutions" gives detailed advice on changing yarns; "Tips & Tricks" introduces easy techniques to simplify or tidy your work; "Knitting Bag" covers my favorite essential notions; and "iKnit" includes my favorite iPhone and iPad apps.

You can find additional techniques, references, and resources in the Epilogue.

Substitutions

When substituting yarn from your stash, it's important not only to consider the gauge but also the unique qualities of the fiber and yarn construction. To that end, each pattern includes a photo of the yarn and a brief description of its construction or quality. Because a small swatch often won't showcase the nature of a given yarn over a much larger piece of work (particularly shawls or full-sized garments), for comparable knitted results, try to use similar fibers and yarn construction as well as similar gauge.

Alternatively, select a different fiber or blend to produce different results. Swap a solid for a hand-dye for crisper stitches; a fuzzy for a gentle halo or worn look; or a multicolored handspun for a commercial solid to add color interest and visual texture to a plain pattern. Just keep in mind the traits you need to preserve for fit (namely, memory versus drape) and that patterns knit at a very tight gauge (for example, a worsted knit on 3s) are more forgiving of substitutions than those knit at a loose gauge or the ball-band gauge.

Basic Fiber Qualities

Keep these characteristics in mind when making substitutions:

- Wool has memory and retains its shape; fine wools such as merino have the most memory and bounce, whereas more robust, scratchier wools have a firmer body and are sturdier.
- Superwash wool tends to have more drape and less memory than an equivalent

non-superwash option; it's also a bit heavier for a similar length/gauge, resists pilling, and its smooth surface gives nice stitch definition.

- Silk, soy silk, bamboo, and TENCEL® provide drape and luster, but they lack memory.
- Cotton, linen, and hemp have drape and breathe well, but they lack memory.
- Alpaca provides extra warmth, drape and a halo; some alpaca is also lustrous.
- Angora adds a halo and much warmth; it tends to get matted with abrasion.
- Nylon adds strength and stability.
- Cashmere is soft and light, but it's not well suited to garments that require memory or face abrasion.
- Mohair adds strength and luster, but it lacks wool's memory.

Basic Yarn Qualities

Like the fiber type, the construction of the yarn itself should inform your substitution.

- Generally speaking, the more plies and the tighter the plies, the more stitch definition and the better a yarn wears.
- Single ply yarns ("singles") soften patterns and usually felt very well.
- Unique construction, such as knit tubes, add extra stability to short or fuzzy fibers by anchoring them into the yarn's base; in smooth fibers, tubes provide nice stitch definition.
- Hand- and kettle-dyed yarns, heathers, and tweeds soften stitch patterns, whereas solids make them pop more.
- Similarly, textured patterns soften the sometimes-hard color lines and stripes produced when knitting with hand-dyed yarns.

Tips & Tricks
Tidy Circular Join

CO required number of stitches and bring end up in the round to join.

slip 1st st from left needle to rt needle

1. Slip first CO st from left needle to right.

bring tail up between needles

1st st

2. Bring tail between first and second sts from the front.

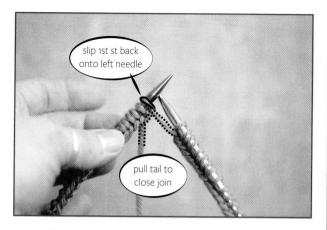

3. Slip st back to left needle.
4. Pull tail to snug join.

2. Insert the needle into the center of the last BO stitch to form and pull through.

Tidy Circular Finish

Thread the tail from the last BO stitch onto a needle.

1. Run the needle under both legs of the first BO stitch and pull through.

3. Adjust so it's the same size as all the other stitches along the edge and weave in ends.

Spit Splicing

This only works with non-superwash animal fibers and high-animal blends (at least half of fiber content should be some form of animal fiber).

1. Break both ends (tapers the ends versus cutting).

2. If working with a multi-ply yarn, break each successive ply at a higher point.

3. Overlap tapered ends in palm of hand, wet with water or spit, and rub palms together to splice ends by felting. Rub gently at first and check positioning, then rub vigorously after you verify that the overlap is nice and even.

4. You're striving for a join that's the same diameter as the rest of the yarn. Test join by tugging lightly before knitting.

Knot Splicing

For fibers that won't spit splice, my current favorite is the double knot or "magic knot." Although this splice isn't completely invisible, it hides well in textured patterns or variegated colors in lightweight yarns. I'm not keen on it for color changes, because it's difficult to predict where the knot will fall, or for heavy yarns, which make a bulky knot that's harder to hide, but it's a real time-saver for single colors when you're working with many small balls and a large project. I haven't been using this splice enough to have complete confidence (I'm more apt to go the traditional route and weave in ends on a very complicated project where an emergency darn would be a nightmare), but so far, I've had no splice failures when I tested the finished knot vigorously beforehand.

I learned this terrifying splice here: www.youtube.com/watch?v=-nq_7EXTWHE.

NOTE: It's very important to test the finished knot by tugging enthusiastically. I've goofed it before, and a good hard tug will break the splice so you can reknot. Better safe than sorry.

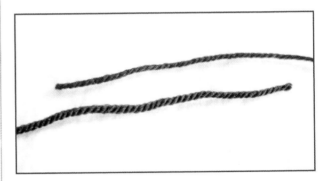

1. Lay the two strands side by side in opposite directions.

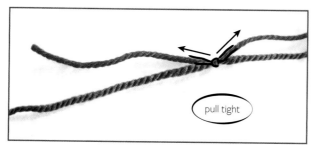

2. Bring the first strand around the second and knot it to itself. Pull tight.

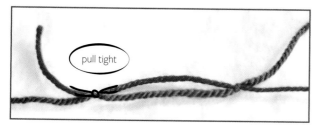

3. Repeat with the other side. Pull tight.

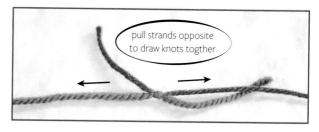

4. Now pull the two working ends firmly in opposite directions to snug the two knots together.

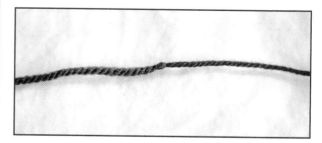

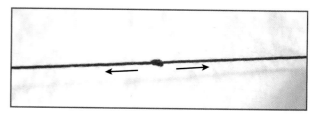

5. Trim the tails very close to the knot with sharp, small scissors, being careful not to nick the knot itself. Tug firmly several times to test the knot, and start over if it fails.

Multi-Strand Weave

For those cases where you don't want to use a magic knot but can't spit splice, unraveling the ends and weaving in each ply separately minimizes bulk and produces a more stable weave. For slippery fibers, using a sharp embroidery needle to split the yarn on the wrong side (rather than duplicating the path of the knitting), and then doubling back on your weave further stabilizes stitches.

Slipped Stitch Edging

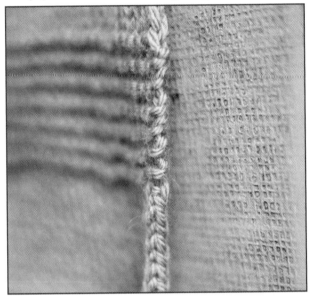

Regular edge

Slipped stitch edge

Because it looks clean and is easier to pick up through, I almost always use a slipped-stitch edging. No matter what the rest of the pattern, slip the first stitch and knit the last stitch of every row.

Pick Up through Slipped Stitch Edge

You can pick up through one or both legs of the slipped-stitch edge, or start with the RS or WS to vary the look of the pick up edge. Most of my patterns call for a specific pick up starting from a specific side. If the type is not specified, assume pick up through both legs.

From RS, pick up through both legs.

From RS, pick up through close leg only.

Mind the Gap

Handy for any gusset/3D shaping (thumbs, heels, sleeves, and so on). Whenever you have any kind of crotch forming (two angled 3D pieces coming together like a branching tree), the transition often forms a hole at the joint. To avoid this hole, pick up a stitch a row or two *below* the gap (between the two planes formed by the crotch). Depending on the size of the gap, you might pick up an extra stitch and decrease them on the next rnd.

The Knitting Bag

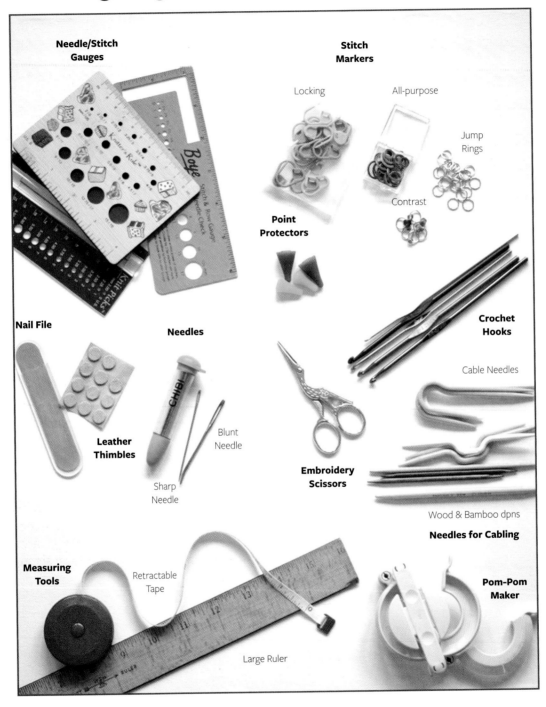

Needle/Stitch Gauges

Stitch Markers

Locking

All-purpose

Jump Rings

Contrast

Point Protectors

Crochet Hooks

Nail File

Needles

Cable Needles

Leather Thimbles

Blunt Needle

Embroidery Scissors

Sharp Needle

Wood & Bamboo dpns

Needles for Cabling

Measuring Tools

Retractable Tape

Pom-Pom Maker

Large Ruler

All-Purpose Stitch Markers

Lots of them—the plainer and thinner, the better. My favorites are Susan Bates Wafer-Thin Stitch Count Markers. I also like the plain jump rings from the jewelry section of the craft store.

Contrast Stitch Markers

These stand out to mark your round or other important section. I prefer the plainer type without dangles or curlicues that interfere with my work. Search www.etsy.com for "snagless stitch markers."

Locking Stitch Markers

To add after the fact or mark a spot to measure. Clover Locking Stitch Markers are my favorite. If you're a minimalist, use these for contrast markers, too.

Needle/Stitch Gauge

Pick one that also has a stitch gauge or ruler marks.

Measure Tape or Ruler

I prefer a 12" or 18" flat ruler when I'm at home, but a retractable tape is handier on the go.

Leather Thimble Pads

Colonial Needle ThimblePads (about $7.00 for 12) were designed for quilting, but are a godsend if you push off with your finger while you knit, especially with fine lace needles or the stabby Knit Picks needles. They're self-adhesive and reusable, and each one lasts for months. Stick your active one to your yarn gauge, vinyl notions bag, or any other non-porous surface when not in use.

Embroidery Scissors

Sharp, pointy, and wee enough to fit in tiny knitting bags, embroidery scissors are much more precise for close yarn cuts, and especially nice for a knot splice.

Crochet Hooks

Assorted sizes for working dropped stitches, applying edging, chaining cords, or picking up large numbers of stitches along edges (wrap yarn around hook knitwise so the loop is properly oriented on hook; transfer to knitting needles every 15–20 sts).

Needles

I like blunt needles for kitchener stitch and cinching, and sharp needles for weaving in ends. I love my little Clover Chibi case, which comes with two bent-tip needles and has plenty of room for more.

Point Protectors

Good for keeping stitches on your needles. Handy to use with spare circulars instead of scrap yarn to hold sleeves or stitches. (You can substitute rubber bands for point protectors when you're in a pinch.) The silicone point protectors from Clover are my favorites.

Pom-Pom Makers

Kind of frivolous and not part of my must-have notions bag, the ingenious Clover Pom Pom makers with their interconnected flip-up wings come in five different sizes and make pom-pom creation a snap.

Manufacturer Information

Visit the following websites to find the products described in this section:

* **Addi** (www.skacelknitting.com): Knitting needles.
* **Boye** (simplicity.com/t-boye.aspx): Knitting gauge and other notions. Available at knitting stores and national craft chains.
* **ChiaoGoo** (www.chiaogoo.com): Knitting needles.
* **Clover** (clover-usa.com): Locking stitch markers, Chibi yarn needles and case, point protectors, pom-pom makers. Available at knitting stores and national craft chains.
* **Colonial Needle** (colonialneedle.com): Leather Thimble Pads.
* **Etsy** (www.etsy.com): Fancy handmade stitch markers and knitting notions.
* **HiyaHiya** (hiyahiya-usa.com): Knitting needles.
* **KaratStix** (www.etsy.com/shop/karatstix): Adorable bamboo gauges and tools. Custom order your favorite design (I've seen gnomes, chickens, socks, yarn, spindles, sheep, alpacas, etc.—check www.flickr.com/photos/karatstix for ideas).
* **Knit Picks** (www.knitpicks.com): Knitting needles.
* **Susan Bates** (www.coatsandclark.com): Wafer-Thin Stitch Count Markers. Available at knitting stores and national craft chains.

iKnit

My iPad is one of my favorite knitting accessories. Here are some of my favorite knitting apps, all of which are available in the Apple App Store. Most are iPhone apps that also work with the iPad (except as noted).

StitchMinder

StitchMinder is a great basic counter app. Enables you to track four different counts at once. It's great for working simultaneous increases and pattern repeats, or when you're working on multiple projects. (Developed by Quilt2Go. Free.)

Yarn Genie

I use Yarn Genie often for the needle size converter (US/metric/English), but it also includes a yarn estimator for various garments and a "Stash Basher" that calculates general project options based on gauge and yardage. (Developed by Yarnmarket, LLC. Free.)

Lion Brand Yarn

Besides Lion-centric features (yarn and pattern info), this app also includes a nice assortment of how-to videos. (Developed by Orchard Yarn and Thread Company, Inc. Free.)

Knitting Help

This app includes the same great videos that you can find on www.knittinghelp.com, but they're at your fingertips without an Internet connection! (Developed by Outer Limits Media, Inc. $4.99.)

PaperPort Notes (iPad only)

By far my favorite knitting app is not a knitting app at all, but a PDF notation app that works only on the iPad. I use it to mark up and track my spot on PDF patterns and charts. It includes a highlighter (to mark your chart row or highlight your size choice in multiple size patterns), pen, eraser, and type tool. It even enables you to create audio notes. You can save and share your changes—for example, if you want to save your marked-up pattern to your library or save changes when you're working on a custom chart. (Developed by Nuance Communications. Free.)

SketchBook Express and SketchBook MobileX (iPad and iPhone, respectively)

You can use SketchBook Express (for iPad) or SketchBook MobileX (for iPhone) for sketching out your own designs. Alternatively, if your pattern or chart isn't already a PDF, you can snap a photo of it and then mark it up with the Notes app. You can set brush color, diameter, and opacity to make your own highlighter, and you zoom in or out to add detailed notes. (Developed by Autodesk. Free.)

DesignKNIT (iPad only)

DesignKNIT, which works only with the iPad, is a limited (but cheap and easy) knit charting app that enables you to create your own simple pattern charts and export them via jpeg or PDF. At the time this book was written, the app didn't support colorwork, but fingers crossed that it will someday! DesignKNIT is handy for designers or for quickly charting written patterns. (Developed by Core Computing Technologies. $4.99.)

1

In Which We Knit

Women's

Accessories

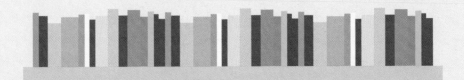

Catherine Bed Socks

Catherine Bed Socks

Wuthering Heights

Confession: I originally read *Wuthering Heights* thanks to Pat Benatar. *Crimes of Passion* was one of my favorite childhood albums, and I figured any story worthy of a Pat B. song (I didn't then know it was actually a Kate Bush cover) was good enough for me.

Back then I viewed Heathcliff as a dark dreamboat—a wronged outsider loner. These days, Heathcliff just seems like a jerk. In fact, *Wuthering Heights* is altogether too moody for me now.

I'm also struck by how the heroines I remembered as wild and fearless actually spend half their time convalescing. And so, I offer these cozy, luxurious, and very Victorian bed socks. (And because *Wuthering Heights* is equally chockablock with sickly boys, you can use this pattern with US 3/3.25mm needles and a gauge of 21 sts × 29 rows for a gents' version, subbing 1×1 ribbing for the eyelets.)

Not intended for the abrasion of shoes, these ultra cushy slipper socks are dreamy for toasting bedtime toes or padding around on lazy winter mornings. Adapted from an antique pattern, they're updated with modern colors and a luxe superwash Merino/cashmere blend yarn.

SIZE
Women's One-Size

MATERIALS
MC: 2 skeins Lion Brand *Superwash Merino Cashmere* (72% superwash Merino/15% nylon/13% cashmere, 87yd./80m per 1.4oz./40g). Shown in #189 Wine.

CC: 2 skeins Lion Brand *Superwash Merino Cashmere*. Shown in #196 Sangria.

Buttery superwash 3-ply where Merino dominates and cashmere adds warmth and a gentle halo.

2 yd. (1.8m) Cam Creations 1¼" (32mm) silk embroidery ribbon (see Epilogue). Shown in #1130 Boysenberry.

US 2 (2.75mm) circular needles, 24" (60mm) length (longer is fine), *or size needed to obtain gauge*

GAUGE
24 sts × 32 rows = 4" (10cm) in St st

Instructions

Edging

Loosely CO 40 sts in CC.

Row 1: Sl 1, knit to end.

Row 2: Sl 1, [k2tog, yo] across row to last 3 sts, k2tog, k1—39 sts.

Row 3: Sl 1, knit to end.

Row 4: Sl 1, purl to last st, k1.

Sock

Slip first stitch and knit last stitch every row.

With MC: Knit 2 rows, purl 1 row, knit 1 row.

With CC: Knit 1 row, purl 1 row.

Repeat last 6 rows until you have 23 stripes of each color, ending with CC stripe.

Toe

Continue to slip first stitch and knit last stitch of every row.

Next row: Cont in CC, sl 1, k1, [k2tog, k2] 9 times, k1—30 sts.

Work 3 rows in St st.

Next row: Sl 1, [k2tog, k1] 9 times, k2tog—20 sts.

Work 3 rows in St st.

Next row: K2tog across row—10 sts. Leave the stitches on your needle and do not cut the yarn.

Top of Foot/Seam

NOTE: If you have large ankles/calves, insert this short row set (see the Epilogue if you need help with short rows) between the third and fourth rows on both sides: Sl 1, k20, wrap and turn work, purl to last st, k1. Continue as directed, knitting in short row wrap on next row.

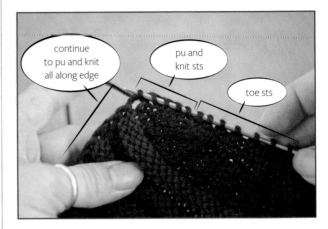

With RS facing and CC, starting at the tapered (toe) end, using the same needle that holds your toe sts, pick up and k75 sts along side edge (1 st for every slipped st along side edge, 3 sts along side edge of toe, and 1 st in every other row along edging).

Row 1: Sl 1, p73, p2tog (last side st and first toe st). Turn work.

Row 2: Slip next toe st onto left needle, k2tog, knit to end.

Row 3: Sl 1, p73, p2tog. Turn work.

Rows 4 & 5: Rep last 2 rows once more—75 side sts, and 5 toe sts rem. Break yarn.

With RS facing and starting from straight (edging) end, using the other end of your needle and CC, pick up and k75 sts along rem side edge (pick up *under* any strands carried along edge), 1 st for every slipped st along edging and sides.

Row 1: Slip next toe st to left needle, p2tog, purl to last st, k1.

Row 2: Sl 1, k73, k2tog. Turn work.

Row 3: Slip next toe st to left needle, p2tog, purl to last st, k1.

Rows 4 & 5: Rep last 2 rows—75 side sts, and no toe sts rem.

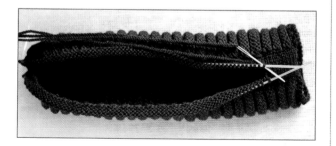

Seam with Kitchener st. (See the Epilogue for information on the Kitchener stitch.)

Weave in ends.

Weave ribbon through eyelets, try sock on, and tie in a bow in front.

Kitty Muff

Anna Karenina

This cozy muff, inspired by the ice-skating scene early in the novel, is sweet, innocent, feminine, and warm—just like Kitty, the bright, sensible foil to the striking but unhappy Anna.

A warm muff is essential if you don't want to hide your outfit under a bulky coat—making it the perfect winter accessory for your favorite fashion plate. With the detachable neck cord, it's perfect for those times when you need both manual dexterity and warmth.

A simple textured check and pretty two-color Latvian braids embellish the pale pink exterior. The optional hidden pocket is worked into the lining using the leftover contrast color from the muff's exterior. Both the interior and exterior are worked in the round, then assembled, with layers of batting between. The joining stitches are picked up through the cast-on and bound-off ends of both layers, with the interior slightly larger so the "fur" lining shows from outside. The muff is finished with a rolled edging and a removable I-cord neck strap.

SIZE
One size fits all

YARN
Exterior MC: 2 hanks Blue Sky Alpacas *Worsted Hand Dyes* (50% royal alpaca/50% merino, 100yd./91m per 3.5oz./100g). Shown in 2008 Light Pink.

Exterior CC: 1 hank Blue Sky Alpacas *Worsted Hand Dyes* (50% royal alpaca/50% merino, 100yd./91m per 3.5oz./100g). Shown in 2003 Ecru.

A strong, soft cable-plied yarn with fantastic stitch definition.

Lining: 4 hanks Blue Sky Alpacas *Brushed Suri* (67% baby suri alpaca/22% merino/11% bamboo, 142yd./130m per 1.75oz./50g). Shown in 900 Whipped Cream.

A very fuzzy, lightweight brushed alpaca yarn.

US 7 (4.5mm) circular needles, 16" (40mm) length, *or size needed to obtain gauge*

US 5 (3.75mm) circular needles, 16" (40mm)

US 5 (3.75mm) for small-diameter knitting (dpns, 2 circulars, or Magic Loop—for optional pocket)

Sharp tapestry needle

4 large safety pins

Full-size scissors to cut batting

2 heavy-duty sew-on snaps (for optional pocket)

Quilt batting

Small d-ring and small swivel latch/clasp (available in sewing or purse notions department of craft stores)

GAUGE

Worsted Hand Dyes: 15 sts × 22 rows = 4" (10cm) in St st on larger needles

Brushed Suri: 14 sts × 21 rows = 4" (10cm)in St st on larger needles with yarn held doubled

Pattern Notes

2-Color Latvian Braid

Wind off 6 yd. (5.5m) of CC into a butterfly. Using a little butterfly that can hang down freely will minimize tangling.

Rnd 1 (Setup): Knit, starting with MC and alternating between MC and CC every stitch.

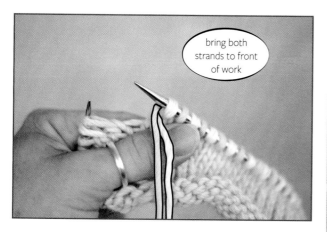

bring both strands to front of work

Rnd 2: Bring both strands to front.

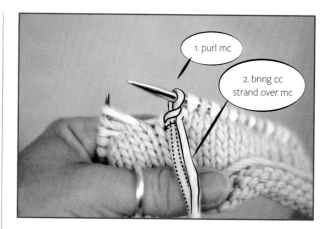

1. purl mc

2. bring cc strand *over* mc

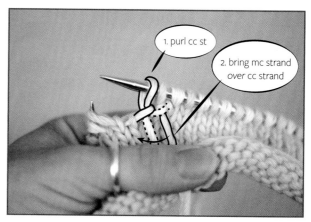

1. purl cc st

2. bring mc strand *over* cc strand

*Bring MC strand over CC strand and purl with MC, bring CC strand over MC strand and purl with CC; rep from * across. *Tip:* To keep strands in good order, I like to let them hang straight down after each stitch and pull the working strand over.

Rnd 3: Rep Rnd 2, except bring the working color under the other color before purling the next stitch.

Instructions

Exterior

With MC and large needles, loosely CO 78 sts. Join for working in the rnd, pm for beg of rnd.

Rnds 1–4: Knit.

Rnds 5–8: *K2, p4; rep from * around.

Rep Rnds 1–8 once more.

Knit 2 rnds.

Work 2-color Latvian Braid.

Knit 2 rnds.

Work 4 rnds of k2, p4 rib.

Knit 4 rnds.

Rep last 8 rnds 4 more times, work 4 rnds of k2, p4 rib, then knit 2 rnds.

Work 2-color Latvian Braid.

Knit 2 rnds.

Work 4 rnds of k2, p4 rib.

Knit 4 rnds.

Rep last 8 rnds once more. BO all sts.

Weave in ends, bathe, and block to about 14" (35.5cm) wide by 8½" (21.5cm) high.

Interior with Pocket

With larger needles and 2 strands of *Brushed Suri*, loosely CO 50 sts. Join for working in the rnd, pm for beg of rnd.

Work 12" (30.5cm) in St st.

BO 14 sts, knit to end—36 sts. Do not turn.

CO 14 sts, knit to end—50 sts. Join to work in the rnd again, pm for beg of rnd.

Work 2½" (6.5cm) in St st.

BO all sts. Weave in ends.

Hidden Pocket

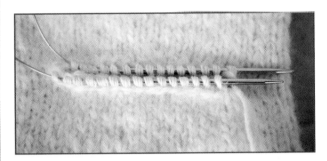

With CC and smaller needles, with RS facing, pick up and knit 14 sts along each edge of opening, and 1 st along each end of opening—30 sts. Join for working in the rnd, pm for beg of rnd.

*[K2, m1] 6 times, k3; rep from * once more—42 sts.

Work St st for 8" (20.5cm).

3-Needle BO: *Working through one st from front needle and one st from back needle, k2tog and BO; repeat from * to end.

Turn piece with WS facing, divide stitches between 2 dpns and close in a 3-needle bind-off, leaving an 8–10" (20.5cm–25.5cm) tail.

Weave in tail on pickup end, and leave BO end tail loose.

Cut a 24" (61cm) length of CC, untwist to separate plies, and use a few plies to sew your snaps into place.

Interior without Pocket

With large needles and 2 strands of *Brushed Suri,* loosely CO 50 sts. Join for working in the rnd, pm for beg of rnd.

Work 14½" (37cm) in St st.

BO all sts. Weave in ends.

To Assemble

Join Tubes

Turn interior tube inside out (knit side to inside) and insert into exterior tube so that WS are together, and matching up CO ends . If you made the hidden pocket, line it up with where the braid jogs (row end) on the exterior tube, so that when it's worn, the jogs will be facing the body, as will the pocket.

Because the two tubes have a different number of stitches, pin them together in four places to keep them lined up evenly while you work.

pu and knit through top loop only of exterior edge and either/both loops of interior edge

Starting with BO edge of exterior tube facing you, using larger needles and CC yarn, and working through both layers, pick up and knit 1 stitch for every stitch on exterior edge. Work just through the top leg of the stitch on the exterior side and whatever is convenient on the interior. The exterior edge needs to be nice and tidy, whereas the interior edge will be obscured both by the fuzzy yarn and by the rolled edging. Because both tubes have different numbers of stitches, you'll

occasionally be working twice through the same interior edge stitch and once through the exterior stitch. For these, work one of the stitches through just the top loop of the edge and the other through both loops.

Rolled Edging

When you've picked up 78 sts, wrap the next stitch as you would for a short row and turn work (this joins the stitches so you can work in the round), pm for beg of rnd.

Change to smaller needles. Knit 6 rnds, then BO.

The purl side will naturally curl up to form a rolled edging.

Stuff Muff

Cut a 15 × 44" (38 × 112cm) piece of quilt batting. Fold in half twice to form a doubled tube and baste ends closed to form an 11 × 15" (28 × 38cm) rectangle when flattened.

Open up piece along free ends with WS of both pieces showing. Insert interior tube into batting tube. If you made the pocket version, tack down pocket to WS of interior tube with tail first.

Turn exterior tube back over interior tube and over batting (most of the stretching will be width-wise).

Close and Edge Other Side.

Line up CO ends and, keeping stuffing inside, pin ends together.

Join ends and work rolled edge as before, working through only top loops as you pick up along exterior edge.

Adjust cover so "furry" ends protrude a bit on each side.

With smaller needles and MC, work 40" (101.5cm)of I-cord. Sew one end to latch and one end to ring. Fasten together through muff.

Francie Nolan Tam

A Tree Grows in Brooklyn

Inspired by the poufy tassle-festooned tam-o-shanters of the WWI era, this jaunty tam offers a modest touch of whimsey that is perfect for the imaginative, tenacious young protagonist of *A Tree Grows in Brooklyn*.

Knit of squishy, minimally processed yarn that's kettle-dyed in small batches, the hat is both charmingly rustic and deliciously soft. The tam is shown with a low-key single pom-pom, but the sidebar covers some authentic period variations if you would like to change it up a bit.

SIZE
Adult Woman (flat diameter=11¼" [28.5cm])

YARN
1 skein Wicked Stitch *Cauldron-Dyed Worsted* (100% wool; 140 yd./128m per 3.5 oz./100g). Shown in Goblin.

A soft, bouncy homespun-feel 2-ply in muted, kettle-dyed colors.

US 4 (3.5mm) dpns or 16" (40cm) circular needle

US 8 (5mm) dpns, 16" (40cm) circular needle *and* dpns, or long circular for Magic Loop, *or size needed to obtain gauge*

Tapestry needle

Pom-pom maker (optional)

GAUGE
16 sts × 24 rows = 4" (10cm) in St st on larger needles

Instructions

With smaller needles, CO 80 sts.

Join for working in the rnd, pm for beg of rnd.

Rnd 1: *K1, p1; rep from * around.

Rnd 2: *K3, p1; rep from * around.

Rep last 2 rnds 4 more times.

Change to larger needles.

Rnd 1: *(K1, p1) twice, m1; rep from * around—100 sts.

Rnds 2, 4, & 6: *K3, p2; rep from * around.

Rnds 3, 5, 9, 11: Knit.

Rnd 7: K4, m1, *k5, m1; rep from * to last st, k1—120 sts.

Rnds 8 & 10: *K3, p3; rep from * around.

Rnd 12: K2, m1, *k6, m1; rep from * to last 4 sts, k4—140 sts.

Rnd 13: Purl.

Rnd 14: *P1, sl 1 wyif; rep from * around.

Rnd 15: *Sl 1 wyif, p1; rep from * around.

Rnd 16: Purl.

Rnds 17 & 21: Knit.

Rnd 18: *K4, p3; rep from * around.

Rnd 19: *K2tog, k5; rep from * around—120 sts.

Rnd 20 & 22: *K3, p3; rep from * around.

Rnd 23: *K4, k2tog; rep from * around—100 sts.

Rnds 24 & 26: *K3, p2; rep from * around.

Rnd 25: Knit.

Rnd 27: *K2tog, k3; rep from * around—80 sts.

Rnds 28, 30, & 32: *K2, p2; rep from * around.

Rnds 29, 31, & 35: Knit.

Rnd 33: *K2, k2tog; rep from * around—60 sts.

Rnds 34 & 36: *K2, p1; rep from * around.

Rnd 37: *K2tog, k1; rep from * around—40 sts.

Rnds 38 & 40: *K1, p1; rep from * around.

Rnds 39 & 43: Knit.

Rnd 41: *K2tog; rep from * around—20 sts.

Rnds 42 & 44: *K1, p1; rep from * around.

Rnd 45: *K2tog; rep from * around—10 sts.

Finishing

Break yarn and thread tail through rem sts. Pull tight to secure and fasten off on WS.

Weave in ends.

Finish with a festive 2" (5cm) pom-pom or topping of choice (do soak, press out water, and air-dry finished pom-pom before attaching—this yarn really blooms with a warm soak, so your pom-pom will be much fuller).

Historical Variations

The ladies' tam-o-shanter patterns of the WWI era were quite elaborate! Here are some finishing ideas taken from antique patterns:

* Multiple smaller pom-poms, either attached directly or dangling from I-cord or crocheted tails.
* The same, but with tassles, hanging down like a graduation mortarboard.
* A long tail with a single big fat tassle.
* Decorative pom-poms or crochet flowers along ribbed edging (worn to the side of the face).

Katie Rommely Gaiters

A Tree Grows in Brooklyn

I picture a young, feisty Katie Rommely (or a newly married Katie Nolan), still fresh and hopeful, strolling down a sunny Williamsburg street in these pretty gaiters.

With a deceptively simple 4-row lace pattern and a flared bottom hem, these flat-knit side-button gaiters fan out nicely at the top of the foot and look great with both shoes or boots. An optional pom-pom drawcord adds a playful touch.

SIZE
S/M (L/XL)

MATERIALS
3 skeins Mountain Meadow Wool *Merino Laramie* (100% merino; 196 yd./179m per 3.5oz./100g skein). Shown in Natural.

A soft, bouncy homespun-feel two-ply in natural and dyed colors.

US 7 (4.5mm) needles, *or size needed to obtain gauge*

US 4 (3.5mm) needles

Size F/5 (3.75mm) crochet hook

20 buttons, ⅝" (16mm)–¾" (19mm) width. Shown in La Mode Style 26302.

Needle and button thread

Pom-pom maker (optional)

GAUGE
18 sts × 22 rows = 4" (10cm) in Body patt on larger needles

Instructions

With larger needles, CO 52 (60) sts.

Top Edge

Row 1 (RS): Sl1, *k2, p2; rep from * to last 3 sts, k3.

Row 2: Sl1, p2, *k2, p2; rep from * to last st, k1.

Rep Rows 1 and 2 for 4" (10cm), ending with a WS row.

Eyelet Row: Sl1, *k2, yo, k2tog; rep from * to last 3 sts, k2tog 1 (0) time, k1 (3)—51 (60) sts.

Body

Rows 1 & 3 (WS): Sl1, purl to end.

Row 2 (RS): Sl1, k3, *yo, k2, ssk, k2tog, k2, yo, k1; rep from * to last 2 sts, k2.

Row 4: Sl1, k2, *yo, k2, ssk, k2tog, k2, yo, k1; rep from * to last 3 sts, k3.

Rep last 4 rows 11 more times, then rep Rows 1–3 once more.

Bottom

Row 1 (RS): Sl 1, *k2, p2; rep from * to last 2 (3) sts, m1 (0), k2 (3)—52 (60) sts.

Rows 2, 4, & 6: Sl 1, p2, *k2, p2; rep from * to last st, k1.

Rows 3 & 5: Sl 1, *k2, p2; rep from * to last 3 sts, k3.

Row 7 (Increase Row): Sl 1, *k1, m1, k1, p2; rep from * to last 3 sts, k1, m1, k2—65 (75) sts.

Rows 8–14: Sl 1, work in patt (knitting knit sts and purling purl sts) to last st, k1.

Row 15 (Increase Row): Sl 1, *k1, m1, k2, p2; rep from * to last 4 sts, k1, m1, k3—78 (90) sts.

Rows 16–22: Sl 1, work in patt to last st, k1.

BO loosely in patt.

Button Plackets

With smaller needles and WS facing, pick up and knit 1 st in each slipped stitch along one side edge—49 sts.

Increase Row: Sl 1, [kfb] in each st to last st, k1—96 sts.

Row 1: Sl 1, *p1, sl 1 wyib; rep from * to last st, k1.

Row 2: Sl 1, *k1, sl 1 wyif; rep from * to last st, k1.

Rep Rows 1 and 2 two more times, then rep Row 1 once more.

BO as foll: Sl 1, *k2tog, pass first st over second st and off needle; rep from * to last st, k1, BO. Fasten off rem st.

Rep on other side.

Make second gaiter same as first.

Buttonholes

NOTE: You can easily adjust for a different size or number of buttons by making the crochet chains shorter or longer and by increasing/decreasing the number of crochet slip stitches between buttonholes.

If your first buttonhole seems a bit longer than the others, even after pulling your first st tight, ch 2 instead.

With crochet hook and RS facing, make a slip stitch into the first BO st at the top corner on of the left placket. *Ch 3, skip the next 2 BO sts, work 1 slip st into each of the next 3 BO sts; rep from * to last 3 BO sts, ch 3, skip next 2 BO sts, then work slip st in last BO st. Fasten off.

Rep on second gaiter, this time starting on the bottom corner of the right placket.

Finishing

Weave in ends. Block lace flat. Sew buttons to placket opposite buttonholes.

Optional Pom-pom Drawcord

Make 2 crochet chains or 2-st I-cords 36" (91.5cm) long; do not weave in tails. Soak cords in hot, soapy water for a few minutes, then felt by rubbing the cords between your palms. Make 2 small pom-poms for each cord, thread the cords through the eyelet row, and attach pom-pom to each end.

Meg Mittens

Meg Mittens

Little Women

Though they share the same fundamental DNA, these mittens and the ones in the following pattern are as different in style and character as night and day—or as sisters Jo and Meg March from *Little Women*. Meg's warm, pretty mittens were inspired by a Civil War–era pattern. Like Meg, they're soft, stylish, feminine, and a bit charmingly frivolous. They feature a long, wide brioche stitch cuff; a dainty, ribbon-garnished fitted wrist; a basket-like textured pattern on the hands; and broken rib fingertips and thumb.

These mittens are worked in worsted weight yarn on little needles for a dense, warm fabric. I like to work them two at a time, like socks, with the Magic Loop method.

SIZE
Women's S (M, L)

Hand circumference: 6¾ (7½, 8)" (17 [19, 20.5]cm)

MATERIALS
2 (2, 3) skeins Quince & Co. *Lark* (100% American Wool; 134 yd./123m per 1.75 oz./50g skeins). Shown in Glacier. Plump, lofty, soft 4-ply worsted wool.

US 2 (2.75mm) needles (dpns, 2 short circulars, or 1 long circular for Magic Loop), *or size needed to obtain gauge*

Waste yarn or small stitch holders to hold thumb stitches

Stitch markers

2 locking stitch markers (optional; for 2-at-a-time with Magic Loop)

2 yd. (1.8m) Cam Creations 1¼" (32mm) silk embroidery ribbon (see Epilogue). Shown in Baby Blue #S594.

GAUGE
26 sts × 38 rnds = 4" (10cm) in Sand Stitch

Pattern Notes

Sand Stitch

This is essentially seed stitch, with rows of plain knitting between each K/P row.

Rnds 1 & 3: Knit.

Rnd 2: *K1, p1; rep from * around.

Rnd 4: *P1, k1; rep from * around.

Rep Rnds 1–4 for patt.

Broken Rib

Rnd 1: Knit.

Rnd 2: *P1, k1; rep from * around.

Rep Rnds 1–2 for patt.

Instructions

NOTE: If you're knitting two mittens at once, use a locking stitch marker on the bottom edge to mark your start of round on your *first* mitten. The locking marker will help you keep track of your place because stitch markers will fall off with Magic Loop or two circulars.

TIP: If you're working two mittens at once, wind both hanks together into a single center-pull ball (just knot the two ends together after you wind the first hank, and keep winding) and knit one mitten from the center strand and one mitten from the outside strand. Managing the single ball is far easier than two separate balls.

Cuff

CO 48 (48, 50) sts. Join for working in the rnd, pm for beg of rnd.

Setup rnd: *K1, p1; rep from * around.

Rnd 1: *K1-b, p1; rep from * around.

Rnd 2: *K1, p1-b; rep from * around.

Rep last 2 rnds until piece measures 3½" (9cm) long.

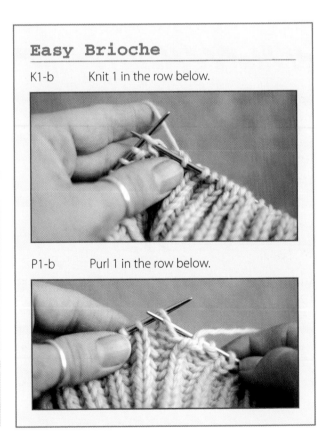

Easy Brioche

K1-b   Knit 1 in the row below.

P1-b   Purl 1 in the row below.

Wrist

Knit 1 rnd.

Rnds 2–4: *K2, p2; rep from * around.

Rnd 5: *Yo, k3tog, k1 (1, 2); rep from * around—36 (36, 40) sts.

Rnd 6: Knit.

Rnds 7–9: Rep Rnds 2–4.

Lower Palm

Rnds 1–8: Work Sand St pattern.

Rnd 9: *K1, m1, k16 (16, 18), m1, k1; rep from * once more—40 (40, 44) sts.

Rnds 10–12: Cont as established, working new Sand Sts into patt.

Rnd 13: K1, m1, (pm size S only), k18 (18, 20), m1, k2, m1, k18 (18, 20), (pm size S only), m1, k1—44 (44, 48) sts.

Rnds 14–16: Cont even in Sand St patt.

Sizes M (L) only:

Rnd 17: K1, m1, pm, k 20 (22), m1, k2, m1, k20 (22), pm, m1, k1—48 (52) sts (markers set off the upcoming thumb sts).

Rnd 18: Work even in patt.

Thumb Gusset

All sizes:

Rnd 1: Knit to marker, m1, sl marker, knit to marker, sl marker, m1, knit to end—46 (50, 54) sts.

Rnd 2: *P1, k1; rep from * around.

Keeping palm sts in Sand St patt, and thumb gusset sts in Broken Rib patt, rep last 2 rnds 6 (8, 10) more times, ending with Rnd 2—58 (66, 74) sts, incl 18 (22, 26) thumb sts.

Upper Palm and Fingers

Next rnd: Knit to 2nd marker, place 18 (22, 26) thumb sts on holder or waste yarn, CO 4 sts over gap—44 (48, 52) sts.

Cont in Sand St patt as established for 16 (20, 28) rnds, then rep Rnds 2 and 3 for 1½" (4cm).

NOTE: If you have longer-than-average fingers, repeat Rnds 1–4 of Sand St patt one additional time before working Rnds 2 and 3 of Sand St patt for 1½" (4cm).

Fingertips

Right now, you have all 4 side stitches along the thumb side at the end of the round, which is why your first decrease round is a little goofy. On the round following your first decrease, you reposition the last stitch onto the beginning of the row, making your decreases balanced from that point on.

Rnd 1: *K1, p1; rep from * around.

Rnd 2: *K18 (20, 22), k2tog, ssk; rep from * once more—40 (44, 48) sts.

Rnd 3: [K1, p1] 9 (10, 11) times, k2, [k1, p1] 9 (10, 11) times, k1, sl 1 to RH needle, remove beg-of-rnd marker, sl st back to LH needle, replace beg-of-rnd marker. This becomes your new start of rnd. (*Note:* If you're working both mittens at once, you'll need to transfer the first one you hit—which is the last stitch of the second mitten—to locking st marker until you work your way back to the start of the mitten on the next round.)

Rnd 4: *Ssk, k16 (18, 20), k2tog; rep from * once more—36 (40, 44) sts.

Rnd 5: *K1, work 16 (18, 20) sts in established Broken Rib patt, k1; rep from * once more.

Rep last 2 rnds 4 (5, 6) more times, working 2 fewer sts between decreases each time—20 sts.

Break yarn, thread tail through rem sts. Pull tight to secure and fasten off on WS.

Thumb

Place thumb stitches on needles. Pick up and knit 6 sts over crotch of thumb (1 st for each CO st, and 1 st at gap on each side of opening), work thumb sts in established patt—24 (28, 32) sts. Join for working in the rnd, pm for beg of rnd.

Rnd 1: Work 16 (20, 24) sts in patt, k2tog, k4, ssk—22 (26, 30) sts.

Rnd 2: Work 16 (20, 24) sts in patt, k2tog, k2, ssk—20 (24, 28) sts.

Rnd 3: Work 16 (20, 24) sts in patt, k2tog, ssk—18 (22, 26) sts.

Rnds 4 & 5: Work even in established Broken Rib patt.

Rnd 6: Work to last 4 sts, k2tog, ssk—16 (20, 24) sts.

Rnds 7–9: Work 3 rnds even.

Rnd 10: Rep Rnd 6—14 (18, 22) sts.

Rnds 11–15: Work 5 rnds even.

Rnd 16: Rep Rnd 6—12 (16, 20) sts.

Rnd 17: Work 1 rnd even.

Rnd 18: Rep Rnd 6—10 (14, 18) sts.

Size S only: End here.

Sizes M & L only:

Rnds 19 & 21: Work even.

Rnds 20 & 22: Rep Rnd 6—10 (14) sts.

Size M only: End here.

Size L only:

Rnds 23 & 25: Work even.

Rnds 24 & 26: Rep Rnd 6—10 sts.

Break yarn, thread tail through rem sts. Pull tight to secure and fasten off on WS. Weave in ends.

Ribbon Trim

Cut ribbon into two 1-yd lengths. Trim ends of ribbon to angles. Weave a ribbon through the eyelets in one mitten's wrist and knot loosely. Repeat for second mitten. Try on mittens before tightening knots—wrist needs to stretch enough for hand to fit through. Tie each ribbon in a neat bow and trim ends to desired length.

Jo Mittens

Jo Mittens

Little Women

As with the sisters they're based on, Jo March's mittens are so different in style and material that you might not immediately guess their relation to Meg's mittens. But look closer and you'll discover that, like the sisters, when you strip away the superficial differences, both have the same excellent character as their basis. Jo's fittingly boyish mittens are a far more practical response to pretty Meg's feminine mittens.

In true tomboy fashion, Jo's mittens are equally appropriate for men. They have a slightly looser fit at the hand and a nice clingy ribbed cuff to keep out the cold and snow. Jo's no-nonsense mittens are worked in sturdy charcoal gray wool. Like Meg's, I like to work them two at a time, like socks, with a Magic Loop.

The M and L sizes here correspond to Men's S/M and M/L, respectively. For a Men's L/XL size, work as for the L size here, substituting US 3 needles at a gauge of 18 sts/30 rnds per 4".

SIZE

Women's S (M, L)

Hand circumference: 8 (8¾, 9½)" (20.5 [22, 24]cm).

NOTE: M and L sizes correspond to a Unisex/Men's S/M and M/L, respectively. Adjust length as necessary to fit.

MATERIALS

1 (1, 2) ball(s) Valley Yarns *Northampton* (100% wool; 247 yd./226m per 3.5oz./100g ball). Shown in 06 Dark Grey.

Classic 4-ply worsted in sturdy wool.

US 2 (2.75mm) needles (dpns, 2 circulars, or 1 long circular for Magic Loop), *or size marked to obtain gauge*

Waste yarn or small stitch holders to hold thumb stitches

Stitch markers, incl 1 locking st marker if using Magic Loop

GAUGE

22 sts × 35 rnds = 4" (10cm) in sand stitch

Pattern Notes

Sand Stitch

This is essentially Seed Stitch, with rows of plain knitting between each K/P row.

Rnds 1 & 3: Knit.

Rnd 2: *K1, p1; rep from * around.

Rnd 4: *P1, k1; rep from * around.

Rep Rnds 1–4 for patt.

Broken Rib

Rnd 1: Knit.

Rnd 2: *P1, k1; rep from * around.

Rep Rnds 1–2 for patt.

Instructions

Cuff

CO 45 (45, 48). Join for working in the rnd, pm for beg of rnd.

Rnd 1: *K3, p2 (2, 3); rep from * around.

Rep Rnd 1 until piece measures 2" (5cm) from beg.

Wrist

Next rnd: *K1, k2tog, p2 (2, 3); rep from * around— 36 (36, 40) sts.

Next 3 rnds: *K2, p2; rep from * around.

Lower Palm

Rnds 1–8: Work in Sand St patt.

Rnd 9: *K1, m1, k16 (16, 18), m1, k1; rep from * once more—40 (40, 44) sts.

Rnds 10–12: Cont as established, working new sts into patt.

Rnd 13: K1, m1 (pm size S only), k18 (18, 20), m1, k2, m1, k18 (18, 20), (pm size S only), m1, k1— 44 (44, 48) sts.

Rnds 14–16: Cont even in patt.

Sizes M (L) only:

Rnd 17: K1, m1, pm, k20 (22), m1, k2, m1, k20 (22), pm, m1, k1—48 (52) sts (markers set off the upcoming thumb sts).

Rnd 18: Work even in patt.

Thumb Gusset

All sizes:

Rnd 1: Knit to marker, m1, sl marker, knit to marker, sl marker, m1, knit to end—46 (50, 54) sts.

Rnd 2: *P1, k1; rep from * around.

Keeping palm sts in Sand St patt, and thumb gusset sts in Broken Rib patt, rep last 2 rnds 6 (8, 10) more times, ending with Rnd 2—58 (66, 74) sts, incl 18 (22, 26) thumb sts.

Upper Palm and Fingers

Next rnd: Knit to 2nd marker, place 18 (22, 26) thumb sts on holder or waste yarn, CO 4 sts over gap— 44 (48, 52) sts.

Cont in Sand St patt as established for 24 (28, 36) rnds, then rep Rnds 2 and 3 for ½" (1.3cm).

NOTE: If you have longer-than-average fingers, repeat Rnds 1–4 of Sand St pattern one additional time before working Rnds 2 and 3 of Sand St pattern for ½" (1.3cm).

Fingertips

Right now, you have all 4 side stitches along the thumb side at the end of the round, which is why your first decrease round is a little goofy. On the round following your first decrease, you'll reposition the last stitch onto the beginning of the row, making your decreases balanced from that point on.

Rnd 1: *K1, p1; rep from * around.

Rnd 2: *K18 (20, 22), k2tog, ssk; rep from * once more—40 (44, 48) sts.

Rnd 3: [K1, p1] 9 (10, 11) times, k2, [k1, p1] 9 (10, 11) times, k1, sl 1 to RH needle, remove beg-of-rnd marker, sl st back to LH needle, replace beg-of-rnd marker. This becomes your new start of rnd.

NOTE: If you're working both mittens at once, you'll need to transfer the first one you hit—which is the last stitch of the second mitten—to a locking st marker until you work your way back to the start of the mitten on the next round.)

Rnd 4: *Ssk, k16 (18, 20), k2tog; rep from * once more—36 (40, 44) sts.

Rnd 5: *K1, work 16 (18, 20) sts in established patt, k1; rep from * once more.

Rep last 2 rnds 4 (5, 6) more times, working 2 fewer sts between decreases each time—20 sts.

Break yarn, thread tail through rem sts. Pull tight to secure and fasten off on WS

Thumb

Place thumb stitches on needles. Pick up and knit 6 sts over crotch of thumb (1 st in each CO st, and 1 st in gap on each side of opening), work thumb sts in established patt—24 (28, 32) sts. Join for working in the rnd, pm for beg of rnd.

Rnd 1: Work 18 (22, 26) sts in patt, k2tog, k4, ssk—22 (26, 30) sts.

Rnd 2: Work 18 (22, 26) sts in patt, k2tog, k2, ssk—20 (24, 28) sts.

Rnd 3: Work 18 (22, 26) sts in patt, k2tog, ssk—18 (22, 26) sts.

Rnds 4 & 5: Work even in established patt.

Rnd 6: Work to last 4 sts, k2tog, ssk—16 (22, 24) sts.

Rnds 7–9: Work 3 rnds even.

Rnd 10: Rep Rnd 6—14 (18, 22) sts.

Rnds 11–15: Work 5 rnds even.

Rnd 16: Rep Rnd 6—12 (16, 20) sts.

Rnd 17: Work 1 rnd even.

Rnd 18: Rep Rnd 6—10 (14, 18) sts.

Size S only: End here.

Sizes M & L only:

Rnds 19 & 21: Work even.

Rnds 20 & 22: Rep Rnd 6—10 (14) sts.

Size M only: End here.

Size L only:

Rnds 23 & 25: Work even.

Rnds 24 & 26: Rep Rnd 6—10 sts.

Break yarn, thread tail through rem sts. Pull tight to secure and fasten off on WS. Weave in ends.

Daisy Cloche

The Great Gatsby

I love that first glimpse of Daisy in *The Great Gatsby*, when she and Jordan are so light and ethereal, floating, airy, without substance, but charmed and charming. Later on, though, Daisy kind of becomes a drag, and is kind of hard to like, but she still does always *look* good. The cloche inspired by Daisy is complicated but seemingly effortless, like the careless class she embodies.

Based on the Jazz Age standby, this stylish cloche is seamlessly shaped with short rows and accented with changing stitch patterns combined with repeating bound-off edges. It is fitted, but not clingy, and you can wear it with or without the rippled velvet band.

SIZE
Women's, One Size Fits All

MATERIALS
2 skeins Quince and Co. *Lark* (100% American Wool; 134 yd./123m per 1.75 oz./50g skein). Shown in Honey.

Plump, lofty, soft 4-ply worsted wool.

US 3 (3.25mm) needles, *or size needed to obtain gauge*

US 7 (4.5mm) 16" (40cm) circular needles, dpns, or longer circulars for Magic Loop method, *or size needed to obtain gauge*

Stitch markers

1 yd. (1m) 1" (2.5cm) black velvet ribbon or belting (optional)

GAUGE
30 sts × 48 rnds = 4" (10cm) in Linen Stitch on larger needles

30 sts × 36 rnds = 4" (10cm) in St st on smaller needles

Pattern Notes

Linen Stitch

NOTE: With an odd number of stitches, as in this pattern, the Linen Stitch will automatically align when worked in the round.

Overview: Alternating knits and stitches slipped with the yarn in the front of the work makes a dense, tight fabric.

Worked in the round:

Row 1: *K1, sl 1 wyif ; rep from *.

Row 2: *Sl 1 wyif , k1; rep from *.

Repeat Rows 1 and 2 for pattern.

Worked flat (used for short rows):

Row 1 (RS): *K1, sl 1 wyif; rep from *.

Row 2 (WS): *P1, sl 1 wyib; rep from *.

NOTE: You can find instructions for short rows in the Epilogue.

Instructions

Brim

With larger needles, CO 125 sts. Join for working in the rnd and pm for beg of rnd.

Work 3 rnds in Linen St.

Short-row Section on Linen Stitch Brim

NOTE: *Linen Stitch is such a dense stitch that short-row wrapping and working in wraps are unnecessary.*

Short Row Set 1 (RS): Work 44 sts in Linen St, turn with WS facing, work back to marker in Linen St. Do not turn.

Repeat, starting on WS. Turn with RS facing.

Work 1 rnd even.

Short Row Set 2 (RS): Work 49 sts, turn with WS facing, work back to marker. Do not turn.

Repeat, starting on WS. Turn with RS facing.

Work 1 rnd even.

Short Row Set 3 (RS): Work 54 sts, turn with WS facing, work back to marker. Do not turn.

Repeat, starting on WS. Turn with RS facing.

Work 1 rnd even.

Repeat Short Row Sets 1 and 2, including rnds worked even.

Rest of Brim

NOTE: Because this dense fabric is knit on larger needles than the St st section to follow, gently snugging up the stitches as you bind them off makes the edge tidy and suitably sized to pick up stitches with smaller needles in the next section.

Continue in Linen St until brim measures 4½" (11.5cm) from CO edge, measured at marker.

BO in pattern, snugging each stitch gently and leaving remaining stitch on the needle.

Main Hat

NOTE: Because the brim folds up, you'll work the main body of the hat from the opposite side of the work.

Turn work so WS of brim is facing.

Change to smaller needles. Working through the BO sts along the edge, pick up and knit 109 more sts—110 sts total, including initial stitch. (*Hint:* Skip every 8th st when picking up.) Join for working in the rnd and pm for beg of rnd.

Work in St st until piece measures 1" (2.5cm) from pick-up rnd.

Short-row Section on Hat Body

NOTE: The folded brim will cover this section, so short row wraps aren't necessary.

Short Row 1 (RS): Knit 95, turn.

Short Row 2 (WS): Purl 80, turn.

Short Row 3: Knit 75, turn.

Short Row 4: Purl 70, turn.

Short Row 5: Knit 65, turn.

Short Row 6: Purl 60, turn.

Short Row 7: Knit 55, turn.

Short Row 8: Purl 50, turn.

Concentric Circles

NOTE: Picking up stitches through just the back edge of each bound-off stitch creates a nice ridge after each Linen Stitch section, accentuating the circles.

1st Circle

Change to larger needles and beg working in the rnd again. Work 12 rnds in Linen St.

BO in patt, gently snugging up each st and leaving the rem st on the needle.

2nd Circle

Change to smaller needles and pick up and knit 87 more sts (88 total) through the back edge of the BO sts only. (*Hint:* Skip every 5th st.) Pm for beg of rnd.

Knit 3 more rnds.

Change to larger needles. Work 8 rnds in Linen St.

BO in patt, gently snugging up each st and leaving the rem st on the needle.

3rd Circle

Change to smaller needles and pick up and knit 65 more sts (66 total) through the back edge of the BO sts only. (*Hint:* Skip every 4th BO st.) Pm for beg of rnd.

Knit 3 more rnds.

Change to larger needles. Work 6 rnds in Linen St.

BO in patt, gently snugging up each st and leaving the rem st on the needle.

4th Circle

Change to smaller needles and pick up and knit 43 more sts (44 total) through the back edge of the BO sts only. (*Hint:* Skip every 3rd BO st.) Pm for beg of rnd.

Knit 3 more rnds.

Change to larger needles. Work 4 rnds in Linen St.

BO in patt, gently snugging up each st and leaving the last live st on the needle.

Change to smaller needles and pick up and knit 21 more sts (22 total) through the back edge of the BO sts only. (*Hint:* Skip every other BO st.) Pm for beg of rnd.

Knit 1 rnd.

K2tog across rnd. (11 sts rem)

Break yarn and run tail through the rem sts. Pull tight and weave in ends.

Blocking

To block, soak cloche in warm water for 20 minutes. Spin or press out excess water. Fold the brim up and give the hat a good stretch all around, then allow it to dry on a hat form or your own head, blocking or wearing it over another snug-fitting knit cap. Blocking it over another cap will make it fitted without being clingy.

Velvet Band (Optional)

Fold end of ribbon in a zigzag (see photo), tacking each fold down in the center and checking the fit around your head with the cloche in place.

Continue tacking down folds until the band fits around your head with about an inch to spare.

Sew down the end under the zigzags. Try on for fit, then sew through the edges on both sides.

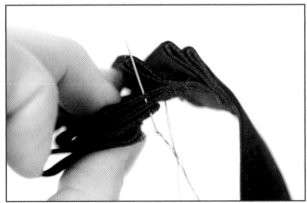

Tess Fingerless Gloves

Tess of the d'Urbervilles

The modern mind has come to imagine Victorian laborers, both industrial and agricultural, as a cast of dull, neutral-swathed extras. But Hardy's flourishes of color and unexpected frills in Tess's pastoral scenes are a refreshing reminder that the "dull extras" in every era are individuals with their own singular whims and styles.

As the pastoral scenes—with their flashes of personal color and taste—testify, the late Victorian period brought colorful garments, previously exclusive to the rich, to everyone. In fact, it's not uncommon to see half a dozen colors used in a single late Victorian knitting pattern because the advent of synthetic dyes in the 1850s brought cheap, colorful textiles to the masses.

These Victorian-flavored fingerless gloves were adapted from a pattern from the era. The simple graphic colorwork detail and geometrical lace have an industrial age feel, making them striking without being overtly feminine or fussy. In fact, we've include a masculine variation (Dorian Gray) suitable for your favorite dandy in Chapter 3.

SIZE
Women's S (M/L)

MATERIALS
MC: 1 skein Louet Gems *Fingering* (100% superwash Merino, 185yd./169m per 1.75oz./50g). Shown in 43 Pewter.

CC: 1 skein Louet Gems *Fingering*. Show in 63 Candy Apple Red.

Soft machine washable high-twist 3-ply with soft luster and excellent definition.

US 1 (2.25mm) and US 2 (2.75mm) needles (dpns, 2 short circulars, or 1 long circular for Magic Loop), *or size needed to optain gauge*

Waste yarn or large safety pin to hold thumb stitches

Stitch markers

GAUGE
32 sts × 44 rnds = 4" (10cm) in St st on smaller needles

Instructions

NOTE: If color isn't specified, work MC.

Trim

With MC and larger needles, CO 72 (90) sts. Join for working in the rnd, pm for beg of rnd.

Rnds 1 & 3: Purl.

Rnd 2: Knit.

Rnd 4: *K1, k2tog, yo; rep from * to end.

Rnds 5, 7, & 9: Knit.

Rnd 6: *Yo, k1, k2tog; rep from * to end

Rnd 8: *K2tog, yo, k1; rep from * to end.

Rnd 10: *K1, k2tog; rep from * to end—48 (60) sts.

Wrist

Change to smaller needles.

Rnds 1–22: Work Colorwork Chart.

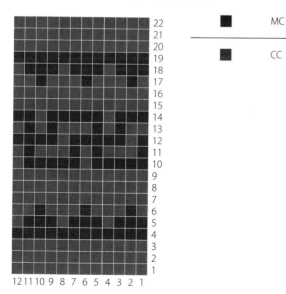

	MC
	CC

Hand

For the hand, divide the stitches evenly into front and back. With 2 short circulars or Magic Loop the division will take care of itself. With dpns, place 24 (30) sts on one needle, and divide the remaining sts between two other needles. After the first rnd, your front (charted) half has an extra stitch.

All the action (both the lace and thumb gusset increases) occur on the odd rounds, whereas all of the even rounds are knit plain.

Right Hand

Rnd 1: Work Rnd 1 of Diamond Lane Chart—49 (61) sts.

Rnd 2 & all even-numbered rnds: Knit.

Rnds 3–13 (odd-numbered rnds only): Work lace pattern on first half of glove; knit to end.

Rnds 15: Work lace pattern on first half; k2, yo, k2, pm, knit to end—50 (62) sts.

Rnd 17–31 (35) (odd-numbered rnds only): Work chart on first half of glove; k2, yo, knit to 2 sts before marker, yo, knit to end—66 (82) sts, with 21 (25) sts in thumb gusset.

Rnd 33 (37): Work chart on first half of glove; place next 21 (25) sts on scrap yarn for thumb, knit to end—45 (57) sts rem for hand.

Rnd 35 (39)–45 (odd-numbered rnds only): Work chart on first half of glove; knit to end.

Left Hand

Rnd 1: Work Rnd 1 of Diamond Lane Chart—49 (61) sts.

Rnd 2 & all even-numbered rnds: Knit.

Rnds 3–13 (odd-numbered rnds only): Work lace pattern on first half of glove; knit to end.

Rnd 15: Work lace pattern on first half; knit to last 4 sts, pm, k2, yo, k2—50 (62) sts.

Diamond Lace Chart

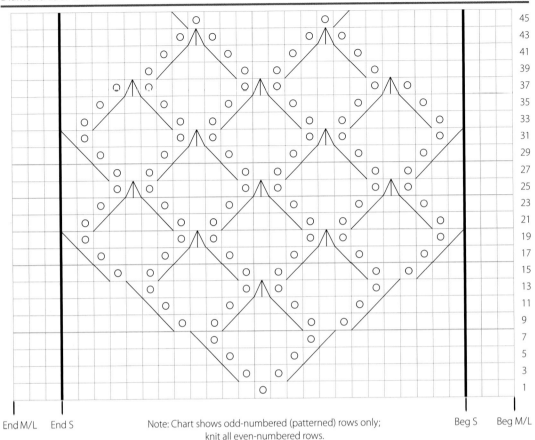

End M/L End S

Note: Chart shows odd-numbered (patterned) rows only; knit all even-numbered rows.

Beg S Beg M/L

45
43
41
39
37
35
33
31
29
27
25
23
21
19
17
15
13
11
9
7
5
3
1

Diamond Lace Chart Key

⋀	sk2p
☐	k
╱	k2tog
╲	ssk
○	yo

Rnd 17–31 (35) (odd-numbered rnds only): Work chart on first half; knit to marker, k2, yo, knit to last 2 sts, yo, k2—66 (82) sts, with 21 (25) sts in thumb gusset.

Rnd 33 (37): Work chart on first half of glove; knit to marker, place next 21 (25) sts on scrap yarn for thumb—45 (57) sts rem for hand.

Rnd 35 (39)–45 (odd-numbered rnds only): Work chart on first half; knit to end.

Top Edge (Both Hands)

Rnds 46 & 47: Knit.

Rnd 48: Knit to last 2 sts, k2tog—44 (56) sts.

Rnds 49–51: Work Rnds 17–19 of Colorwork Chart.

Rnd 52: With MC, knit.

Rnd 53: With MC, purl.

Rnd 54: With CC, knit.

Rnd 55: With CC, purl.

Rnd 56: With MC, BO knitwise.

Thumb

Place thumb stitches to smaller dpns.

With MC, pick up and knit 2 sts over crotch of thumb—23 (27) sts. Join for working in the rnd.

Rnd 1: Knit to 1 st before crotch, k2tog (this becomes your end of rnd)—22 (26) sts. Pm for beg of rnd.

Rnd 2: Ssk, knit to end of rnd—21 (25) sts.

Rnds 3–6: Knit.

Rnd 7: With CC, knit.

Rnd 8: With CC, purl.

Rnd 9: With MC, BO knitwise.

Finishing

Weave in ends. Soak in hot water, press/spin to remove excess water. Lay flat to dry.

2

In Which We Knit

Women's Shawls

and Garments

Emma Shawl

Emma Shawl

Madame Bovary

nspired by spendthrift Emma Bovary, this luxurious featherweight cashmere shawl is knit of thrifty mill ends, hopefully saving you from her impulsive budget woes, if not the whims of her capricious heart.

Though simple enough for book or television knitting, the novel design is fun to knit, as the shawl's shape shifts from round to square to trapezoidal as it's worked. We begin with an arsenic atom forming the circular motif at center (if you're a science geek, feel free to adjust the YO electrons in each purl shell to adapt the design to your favorite element). From there, corner increases worked in the eyelet section produce a squared shape and then two tapered garter wings emerge from the sides to produce a full wrap, which is finished with a modest garter-and-eyelet edge.

SIZE
38" × 72" (96.5 × 183cm)

MATERIALS
1 cone Colourmart *3/28 Heavy Lace* (100% cashmere, 1550 yd./1417m per 5.2oz./150g). Shown in light red.

A soft-spun commercial mill end cashmere 3-ply (mill end color selection changes frequently, so check often for your favorites).

US 4 (3.5mm) dpns + 32" (80cm) circular, *or size needed to obtain gauge*

US 7 (4.5mm) needle or crochet hook, for BO

Stitch markers

GAUGE
20 sts × 30 rows = 4" (10cm) in stockinette

Instructions

Arsenic Atom

With dpns, CO 9 sts.

Join for working in the rnd, pm for beg of rnd.

Rnd 1: Knit.

Nucleus

Rnd 2: *Kfb; rep from * around—18 sts.

Rnds 3 and 5: Knit.

Rnd 4: *K1, p1; rep from * around.

Rnd 6: Rep Rnd 2—36 sts.

Rnd 7: *P1, k1; rep from * around.

Rnds 8, 10 and 12: Knit.

Rnd 9: *K1, p1; rep from * around.

Rnd 11: Rep Rnd 7.

Rnd 13: Rep Rnd 2—72 sts.

Rnd 14: Rep Rnd 7.

Rnds 15 and 17: Knit.

Rnd 16: Rep Rnd 9.

Rnds 18–29: Rep Rnds 14–17 three times.

Rnd 30: *Kfb; rep from * around—144 sts.

Rnds 31 and 32: Purl.

Rnds 33–43: Knit.

First Shell

Rnd 44: P68, p2tog, (yo) twice, p70, p2tog, (yo) twice, p2—146 sts.

Rnd 45: *K67, ssk, kfbf in double yo, k2tog; rep from * once more—144 sts.

Rnds 46–55: Knit.

Rnd 56: *Kfb; rep from * around—288 sts.

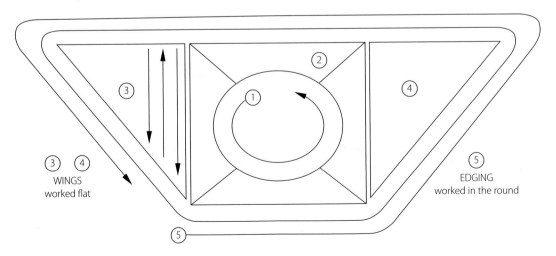

①   ②
ATOM + SQUARE
worked in the round

③   ④
WINGS
worked flat

⑤
EDGING
worked in the round

Second Shell

Rnd 57: P32, p2tog, (yo) twice, *p34, p2tog, (yo) twice; rep from * 6 more times, p2—296 sts.

Rnd 58: *K31, ssk, kfbf in double yo, k2tog: rep from * around—288 sts.

Rnds 59–68: Knit.

Third Shell

Rnd 69: P12, p2tog, (yo) twice, *p14, p2tog, (yo) twice; rep from * 16 more times, p2—306 sts.

Rnd 70: *K11, ssk, kfbf in double yo, k2tog; rep from * around—288 sts.

Rnds 71–80: Knit.

Fourth Shell

Rnd 81: P56, p2tog, (yo) twice, *p55, p2tog, (yo) twice; rep from * 3 more times, p2—293 sts.

Rnd 82: K55, ssk, kfbf in double yo, k2tog, *k52, ssk, kfbf in double yo, k2tog; rep from * around—288 sts.

Rnds 83–104: Knit.

Eyelet Square

Rnd 105: *K2, yo; rep from* around—432 sts.

Rnd 106: *K108, pm; rep from * twice more, knit to end.

Rnd 107: Knit.

Rnd 108: *Kfb, knit to 1 st before marker, kfb; rep from * 3 more times—440.

Rnds 109, 113, 117, 121: Knit.

Even rnds 110–124: *Kfb, knit to 1 st before marker, kfb; rep from * 3 more times—8 sts increased each rnd.

Rnd 111: *K6, yo, k2tog; rep from * around.

Rnd 115: *K4, [yo, k2tog, k6] to marker; rep from * 3 more times.

Rnd 119: K2, *yo, k2tog, k6; rep from * to last 6 sts, yo, k2tog, k4.

Rnd 123: *[Yo, k2tog, k6] to 4 sts before marker, yo, k2tog, k2; rep from * 3 more times.

Rnds 125–158: Rep Rnds 109–124 twice, then rep Rnds 109 and 110 again—640 sts; 160 sts in each section.

(For a square shawl, skip wings and jump to the "Edging" section now.)

Left Wing

Leaving all sts on the needles, work one side of the square only back and forth, decreasing along the bottom edge to form a triangle:

Row 1 (WS): Knit to last 2 sts, k2tog—1 st decreased.

Row 2 (RS): Ssk, knit to end—1 st decreased.

Rep Rows 1 and 2 until 2 sts rem, then BO 1—1 st rem. Do not break yarn.

Next row: Turn work with RS facing and pick up and knit 79 sts (1 st for every 2 rows) from rem st at end of left wing, across bottom edge of left wing, pm, knit 160 sts along bottom edge of square, pm.

Right Wing

Leaving all sts on the needles, work next side of the square only back and forth, decreasing along the bottom edge to form a triangle:

Row 1 (RS): Ssk, knit to end—1 st decreased.

Row 2 (WS): Knit to last 2 sts, k2tog—1 st decreased.

Rep Rows 1 and 2 until 2 sts rem, then BO 1—1 st rem. Pm for beg of rnd.

Next row: With RS facing, pick up and knit 79 sts (1 st for every 2 rows) from rem st at end of right wing across top edge of right wing, pm, knit 160 sts along top edge of square, pm, then pick up and knit 79 sts (1 st for every 2 rows) across top edge of left wing, pm. Kfb in st at point of left wing, then knit across bottom edge of left wing and bottom of square, pick up and knit 79 sts (1 st for every 2 rows) across bottom edge of right wing, kfb in last st—640 sts. Join for working in the rnd.

Edging

Rnd 1: Purl.

Rnd 2: *Kfb, knit to marker, kfb; rep from * around—16 st increased.

Rnds 3 and 4: Rep Rnds 1 and 2—672 sts.

Rnd 5: *K2tog, yo; rep from * around.

Rnds 6–11: Rep Rnd 2 once, rep Rnds 1 and 2 twice, then rep Rnd 1 once more—720 sts.

Rnd 12: *K1, yo; rep from * around—1440 sts.

BO loosely, using larger needle or hook.

Finishing

Soak, press or spin out excess water, and block to about 72" (183cm) wide from tip to tip × 38" (96.5cm), long from top to bottom, allowing center of shawl to curve to preserve arsenic atom's round shape. When blocking, pin along last purl row rather than outside, preserving lettuce edging from final increase round/BO.

Elizabeth Bennet
Summer Blouse

Elizabeth Bennet Summer Blouse

Pride and Prejudice

With her spirit, wit, and good judgment in the face of silly nonsense, Elizabeth Bennet is everyone's favorite romantic heroine.

Feminine but not too frivolous (like our heroine), this Regency-inspired summer top features a tailored back, low-cut, fitted bust, Empire waist, and ruched neckline. The shoulders are worked flat until a broad bustline is cast on and worked in the round to the hem. The bust is shaped with short rows and light gathers. Four rows of alternating eyelets are woven with ribbon to form the Empire waist. The top is finished with contrast ruching.

SIZE
Women's S (M, L, XL)

MATERIALS
MC: 4 (5, 6, 7) skeins Blue Sky Alpacas *Skinny Cotton* (100% organic cotton; 150yd./137m per 2.3oz./65g). Shown in 316 French Blue.

CC: 1 skein Blue Sky Alpacas *Skinny Cotton*. Shown in 30 Birch.

A smooth, finely-plied cotton with a soft sheen.

14–18 yd. (13–16.5m) (longer for longer ribbon tails) 1¼" (32mm) Cam Creations Silk Embroidery Ribbon. Shown in S594 Baby Blue and S052 Bisque.

US 4 (3.5mm) 24" (60cm) circular needles, *or size needed to obtain gauge*

US 4 (3.5mm) dpns or long circular needles for Magic Loop

US 3 (3.25mm) spare needle, for a portion of the BO

Safety pins

Locking stitch markers (6)

GAUGE
18 sts × 27 rows = 4" (10cm) in St st

Instructions

NOTE: This garment has stretch and is designed to be close fitting, so the bust and waist measurements will be 4" to 6" (10–15cm) less than your natural measurements. For reference, the sample shows a size M on a model wearing a 36C pushup bra.

Yoke

CO 29 (33, 37, 41).

Row 1 (RS): K4, pm, k21 (25, 29, 33), pm, k4.

Row 2 and all other WS rows: Purl.

Row 3 and all other RS rows to bustline: K2, yo, *knit to 1 st before marker, yo, k2, yo; rep from * once more, knit to last 2 sts, yo, k2—6 sts increased each RS row.

Rep last 2 rows 20 (25, 30, 36) more times, ending with a RS row—155 (189, 223, 263 sts, with 63 (77, 91, 107) sts for back and 46 (56, 66, 78) sts in each sleeve. Do not turn at end of last row.

Bustline

With RS still facing, pm, CO 65 (79, 93, 109) sts, then pm, join for working in the rnd, knit back and sleeve sts—220 (268, 316, 372) sts. The marker right before your new CO sts becomes your rnd marker.

Next rnd: Knit 65 (79, 93, 109) front sts, place 46 (56, 66, 78) sleeve sts on scrap yarn, knit 63 (77, 91, 107) back sts, place 46 (56, 66, 78) sleeve sts on scrap yarn, leaving end marker in place—128 (156, 184, 216) sts.

Next rnd: K1, [yo, k2tog] across front, knit across back sts.

Back Shaping

Next rnd: Knit to side marker, k18 (22, 27, 31) st, ssk, pm, k2tog, k19 (25, 29, 37), ssk, pm, k2tog, k18 (22, 27, 31) sts—4 sts decreased.

Continue St st and decrease on either side of both back markers every 6th rnd 4 (4, 5, 5) more times.

Bust Short Row Shaping

NOTE: For help with short rows, see Epilogue.

At the same time, when front measures 2" (5cm) from CO edge, begin short row sets over the front sts on the next round. Work 1 (2, 3, 4) full set(s). If you have larger-than-average breasts for your size, work additional set(s) as needed.

Short Row Set

*Knit to 5 sts before side marker. Wrap and turn.

Purl to 5 sts before side marker. Wrap and turn.

Knit to 10 sts before side marker. Wrap and turn.

Purl to 10 sts before side marker. Wrap and turn.

Knit to 15 sts before side marker. Wrap and turn.

Purl to 15 sts before side marker. Wrap and turn.

Knit 1 rnd over all sts to beg-of-rnd marker. Knit 1 rnd, knitting in all wraps, and working back decreases at back dart markers every 6th rnd as before.* Rep from * to * for the short row set.

When you've finished your short row sets, place locking marker through fabric near end of rnd marker. Work another 2" (5cm) from locking marker, maintaining back decreases.

Bust Decreases

Next rnd: K10 (13, 16, 19), [k2tog] 7 (8, 9, 10) times, k17 (21, 25, 31), [ssk] 7 (8, 9, 10) times, k10 (13, 16, 19); knit to end.

Next rnd: K10 (13, 16, 19), [k2tog] 3 (4, 4, 5) times, k19 (21, 27, 31), [ssk] 3 (4, 4, 5) times, k10 (13, 16, 19); knit

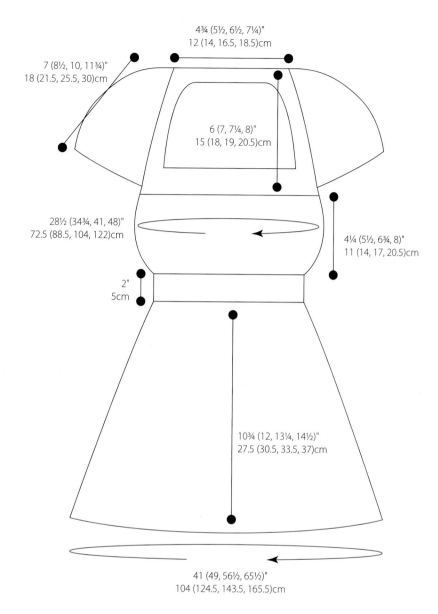

4¾ (5½, 6½, 7¼)"
12 (14, 16.5, 18.5)cm

7 (8½, 10, 11¾)"
18 (21.5, 25.5, 30)cm

6 (7, 7¼, 8)"
15 (18, 19, 20.5)cm

28½ (34¾, 41, 48)"
72.5 (88.5, 104, 122)cm

4¼ (5½, 6¾, 8)"
11 (14, 17, 20.5)cm

2"
5cm

10¾ (12, 13¼, 14½)"
27.5 (30.5, 33.5, 37)cm

41 (49, 56½, 65½)"
104 (124.5, 143.5, 165.5)cm

to end—88 (112, 134, 162) sts rem when all shaping is complete.

Knit 1 rnd even.

Empire Band

Before you get started, count and record the number of sts between your beg-of-rnd marker and your first back decrease marker (#A) and the number between the two back decrease markers (#B). By knowing these two numbers, you can safely drop all other markers (except beg-of-rnd marker!) and avoid fiddling with them; otherwise, all of your markers except your beg-of-rnd marker would get shifted around by the eyelet pattern in the next section,.

Rnds 1 & 9: *K2tog yo; rep from * around.

Rnds 5 & 13: *Yo k2tog; rep from * around.

Rnds 2–4, 6–8, and 11–12: Knit.

Rnds 14 and 15: Knit.

Continue St st and increase every 8th rnd 5 (6, 7, 8) more times, then every 12th rnd twice—184 (220, 254, 294) sts. Drop all markers but beg-of-rnd marker.

NOTE: If you have large hips for your size, or simply prefer a looser fit, you can increase every 6th rnd 7 (8, 9, 11) times, then every 10th rnd 2 (3, 3, 2) times to have 208 (256, 290, 330) sts.

Knit 6 rnds even.

Edging

Rnd 1: *K2tog yo; rep from * around.

Rnd 2: *K1 p1; rep from * around.

Rnd 3: Knit.

Rnd 4: *Yo k2tog; rep from * around.

Rnd 5: *P1 k1; rep from * around.

Rnd 6: Knitting the purl sts and purling the knit sts, BO all sts.

Sleeves

Place 46 (56, 66, 78) sleeve sts on dpns or long circular for Magic Loop.

Pick up and k3 sts over the underarm gap—49 (59, 69, 81) sts. Pm and join for working in the rnd. Knit 5 (5, 7, 9) rnds.

Next rnd: *K2tog, yo; rep from * to last st, k1, yo—50 (60, 70, 82) sts.

Work 2 rnds in k1, p1 rib. BO in pattern.

Neckline

With MC and WS facing, begin at left side of front neck, pick up 1 st for each st along the front neck, 1 st for every 2 rows along the right sleeve, 1 st for each st along the back neck edge, then 1 st for every 2 rows

With locking st markers on back side, starting from beg-of-rnd marker, count out #A sts, pm for first back dart marker, count #B sts, pm for second back dart marker, then another #A sts, pm for side. With front facing, count out #A sts from either side marker and pm for front dart markers (front markers will be closer together than back ones).

Hip Increase Darts

Next rnd: *K1, m1, knit to 1 st before marker, m1, k1; rep from * across rnd—12 sts increased.

along the left sleeve—136 (164, 192, 224) sts. Cut MC and turn with RS is facing.

Pm for beg of rnd and join for working in the rnd. Join CC and knit 1 rnd, and pm at each of the 3 remaining corners as you pass them (neck-sleeve joint and bust-sleeve joints).

Rnd 2: *[K1, m1] to 1 st before marker, k1; rep from * 3 more times—264 (320, 386, 440) sts.

Rnds 3–5: *K2tog, knit to 2 sts before marker, ssk; rep from * 3 more times—240 (296, 362, 416) sts.

Rnd 6: [K2tog] around—120 (148, 176, 208) sts.

Next rnd: With smaller dpn, k2tog, pass last st of rnd over resulting dec st, BO front sts to 1 st before marker,

k3tog, change back to larger needle and BO remaining sts.

Finishing

Weave in ends. Block to finished measurements.

If desired, cut two 1-yd. (.9m) lengths of ribbon. Weave each ribbon through sleeve eyelets and tie in a small bow (sleeves shown without ribbon).

Cut remaining ribbon into 3–4 yd. (2.5–3.5m) lengths. Starting slightly off center, leaving a 36"–48" (91.5–122cm) tail, weave ribbons through Empire waist eyelets. Combine all strands and tie in one large bow, or tie separately into multiple small bows.

Galadriel Hooded Dress

The Lord of the Rings

This leaf-dappled, hooded dress was inspired by the wise and beautiful Lady of the Galadhrim, elf queen of Lothlórien in Middle Earth. I chose a woodsy green color, but you might instead work the dress in a golden colorway for the golden leaves of the majestic mallorn trees of Lòrien.

A soft, mottled effect is achieved by combining two very different fingering yarns: one strand of smooth kettle-dyed wool for color variation and one strand of fuzzy brushed alpaca to soften the color shifts and add an ethereal halo.

SIZE
Women's S (M, L, XL)

MATERIALS
3 (4, 4, 5) skeins Araucania *Ranco Solid* (75% wool, 25% nylon; 376 yd./344m per 3.5oz./100g skein). Shown in 126 Cactus.

A smooth 4-ply sock yarn in kettle-dyed variegated "solids."

NOTE: This yarn has been discontinued at press time. If you can't find it, try 6 (8,8,10) skeins Lorna's *Laces Shepherd Sport* (100% superwash merino, 200yd./183m per 2oz./57g skein) in Grant Park or Ascot.

5 (6, 6, 7) skeins Frog Tree Brushed Suri (100% suri alpaca, 218yd./199m per 1.75oz./50g). Shown in color 46.

A featherweight fuzzy brushed suri alpaca 4-ply fingering.

US 8 (5mm) 16" (40cm) and 32" (80cm) circular needle, plus dpns or long circular for Magic Loop, *or size needed to obtain gauge*

US 7 (4.5mm) 16" (40cm) and 32" (80cm) circular needle

Spare US 8 (5mm) or smaller circular needle, 32" (80cm) length

Rubber bands or point protectors

Locking stitch markers

GAUGE
16 sts × 20 rows = 4" (10cm) in St st on larger needles

Instructions

Hood

NOTE: All sizes use the same hood instructions. (See the "Druid Hood Variation" sidebar for a really full, drapey hood.)

With larger 16" (40cm) circular needle and 1 strand of each yarn held together, CO 18.

Starting with a purl row, work 7 rows in St st, maintaining a slipped-stitch edge.

Next (inc) row: Sl 1, k1, m1, knit to last 2 sts, m1, k2—2 sts increased.

Rep last 8 rows twice more—24 sts. Work 7 rows even.

Next (dec) row: Sl 1, k1, ssk, knit to last 4 sts, k2tog, k2—2 sts decreased.

Rep dec row every 6 rows once, every 4 rows once, then every RS row 3 more times—12 sts.

Break yarn.

With RS facing, rejoin yarn at bottom-right corner. With larger 32" (80cm) circular needle, pick up and knit 1 st in each slipped st along side, pm, from rem sts at top work ssk, k8, k2tog, pm, then pick up and knit 1 st in each slipped st along rem side—58 sts.

Next row (WS): Purl.

Next row: Sl 1, knit to 5 sts before marker, [m1, k1] 5 times, knit to marker, [k1, m1] 5 times, knit to end—68 sts.

Rows 1 & 3 (WS): Sl 1, purl to last st, k1.

Row 2 (RS): Sl 1, knit to end.

Row 4: Sl 1, k1, m1, knit to last 2 sts, m1, k2—70 sts.

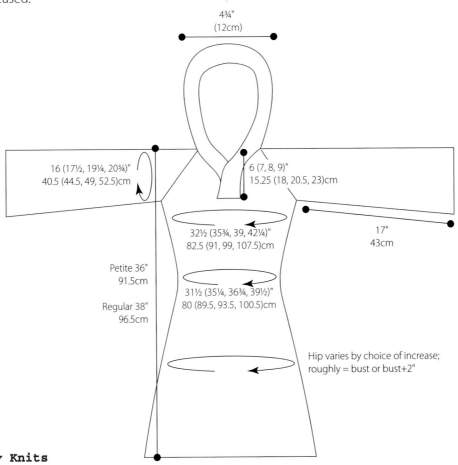

4¾"
(12cm)

16 (17½, 19¼, 20¾)"
40.5 (44.5, 49, 52.5)cm

6 (7, 8, 9)"
15.25 (18, 20.5, 23)cm

32½ (35¾, 39, 42¼)"
82.5 (91, 99, 107.5)cm

17"
43cm

Petite 36"
91.5cm

31½ (35¼, 36¾, 39½)"
80 (89.5, 93.5, 100.5)cm

Regular 38"
96.5cm

Hip varies by choice of increase;
roughly = bust or bust+2"

Rep Rows 1–4 seven more times—84 sts. Place hood sts on spare needle (cap ends with rubber bands or point protectors).

Pick Up Neck

With larger 32" (80cm) circular needle, pick up and knit 1 st in every slipped st along bottom sides of hood and 1 st in every CO st along back section and place markers as follows:

Pick up and k5, pm, pick up and k12, pm, pick up and k18, pm, pick up and k12, pm, pick up and k5, CO 1—53 sts.

Next row (WS): Sl 1, purl to end, CO 1 st—54 sts.

Yoke

Next (inc) row (RS): Sl 1, [knit to 1 st before marker, (kfb) twice] 4 times, knit to end—8 sts increased.

Next row and all WS rows: Sl 1, purl to last st, k1.

Rep last 2 rows 12 more times, then rep RS inc row once more—166 sts. Place rubber bands or point protectors on ends of needles holding yoke sts.

Hood and Yoke edging

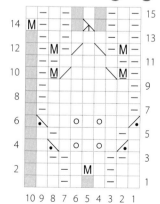

Hood Lace Chart
See end of project for stitch key.

With RS facing, using smaller 32" (80cm) circular needle, pick up and k15 sts through slipped-st edging of yoke, work in patt across hood sts, then pick up and k15 sts through slipped-st edging on the other side of yoke—162 sts.

Rows 1–15: Sl 1, work Hood Lace Chart across hood, ending with K1.

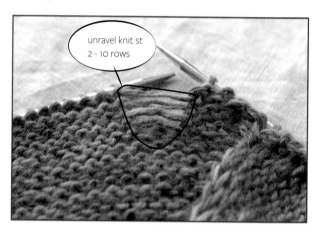

Optional: For a more organic look, with stems of varying lengths, use this trick on the first row of lace (WS). As you reach each knit stitch (which will form your purled stems on RS of work), drop the stitch and unravel it for 2–10 rows to extend the stems down into the hood, then use a crochet hook to "knit" them back up on the WS (the purl side will show on the RS of the hood).

When Hood Lace Chart is complete, BO in pattern, leaving last st live.

Join in the Round

Slip the first st from the yoke off the right needle, place the last st from the lace panel onto the right needle, making sure the working yarn is to the back of the work. Then place the first yoke stitch back on the right needle. Holding both layers of lace inset together, pick up and k9 sts along the edge sts through of both layers of lace panels—176 sts.

Knit around up to 1 st before the lace panel, (k2tog) twice, pm for beg of rnd—174 sts.

Continue St st in the rnd, working raglan increases every other rnd 5 (7, 9, 11) more times—206 (222, 238, 254) sts. 38 (42, 46, 50) rows/rnds have been worked from neck pickup row.

Place Waist/Hip Markers for Shaping

Count in 12 (16, 20, 24) sts in from each sleeve marker and place locking markers on the front and back. These mark your front and back shaping "darts." If you have two different-colored markers, use a different one for the front and back, because they decrease and increase at different rates.

Divide for Sleeves

Removing raglan markers as you come to them, knit to first raglan marker, place 50 (54, 58, 62) sleeve sts on scrap yarn, CO 8 (10, 12, 14) sts, knit across 56 (60, 64, 68) back sts, place 50 (54, 58, 62) sleeve sts on scrap yarn, CO 8 (10, 12, 14) sts, then knit across rem front sts—122 (134, 146, 158) sts.

Waist/Hip Shaping

NOTE: If you're long- or short-waisted, you can adjust to fit your own body.

Read through the following section carefully as decreasing and increasing for front and back happen at different rates.

From this point, you knit all rounds, working the shaping as follows:

On the back: Work to dart marker, sl m, k2tog, knit to 2 sts before next dart marker, ssk, sl m.

On the front: Work to 2 sts before dart marker, ssk, sl m, k2tog, knit to 2 sts before next dart marker, ssk, sl m, k2tog.

Continue in St st and dec at back dart markers on first rnd, then every 6th rnd 6 more times and, **at the same time,** when body measures 3 (3½, 4, 5)" (7.5 [9, 10, 12.5]cm) from armholes, dec on each side of both front dart markers on next rnd, then every 4th rnd 2 (3, 4, 5) more times. Then M1 1 st before first front dart marker and 1 st after second front dart marker every 4th rnd 5 (6, 5, 6) times. **At the same time,** when body measures 16 (17, 17, 18)" (40.5, 43, 43, 45.5]cm) measured from back neck, M1 1 st before and after each back dart marker every 5th rnd 3 (4, 4, 5) times—118 (132, 138, 152) sts. If your hips are on the slimmer side, work the back increase every 6th round instead. If your hips are on the larger side, work an extra increase.

NOTE: If you are making the sweater version of this pattern, jump to the "Lace Hem" section now.

NOTE: Due to alpaca's lack of memory and the garment's length, the dress version could grow a few inches longer over time with wear. If that's an issue, work the stockinette portion a few inches shorter than noted.

Continue inc before first dart marker and after second dart marker of both front and back every 12th rnd 5 (4, 4, 3) times, then work even until dress is 32" (81.5cm) for standard length or 4 (3, 3, 2) times, then work even until dress is 30" (76cm) for petite length, or about 6" (15cm) less than desired final length—138 (148, 154, 164) sts for standard length or 134 (144, 150, 160) sts for petite length.

NOTE: The lace edging adds about 6" (15cm).

Lace Hem

Dress Length:

Knit 1 rnd and inc (dec, inc, dec) 6 (4, 6, 4) sts evenly around for standard length or dec (6, 0, 6, 0) sts for petite length—144 (144, 160, 160) sts for standard length or 128 (144, 144, 160) sts for petite length.

Sweater Length:

Knit 1 rnd and dec (dec, inc, inc) 6 (4, 6, 8) sts evenly around—112 (128, 144, 160) sts.

Work Hem Lace Chart 1—162 (162, 180, 180) sts for standard length dress; 144 (162, 162, 180) sts for petite length dress; or 126 (144, 162, 180) sts for sweater length.

Remove marker, k1, p1, replace marker. Work Hem Lace Chart 2.

BO in patt.

Sleeves

Place held 50 (54, 58, 62) sleeve sts to 16" (40cm) circular needle.

With RS facing and 1 strand of each yarn, pick up and k1 st in gap before CO sts, 8 (10, 12, 14) sts into the CO sts and 1 st in gap after CO sts—60 (66, 72, 78) sts. Join for working in the rnd.

K49 (53, 57, 61), ssk the last sleeve st together with the first underarm st, k8 (10, 12, 14), knit together the last underarm st and first sleeve st—58 (64, 70, 76) sts.

Next rnd: K53 (58, 63, 68), pm for beg of rnd.

Continue St st and dec 1 st at beg and end of every 8th rnd 6 times—46 (52, 58, 64) sts, Work even until sleeve measures 10" (25.5cm) long, measured from armhole. Sleeves will gain 1–1½" (2.5–4cm) in blocking.

Hem/Sleeve Lace Chart 1

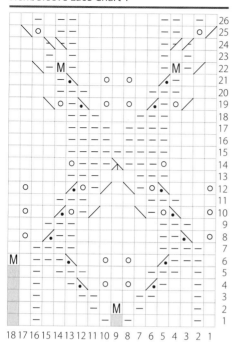

18 17 16 15 14 13 12 11 10 9 8 7 6 5 4 3 2 1

Key

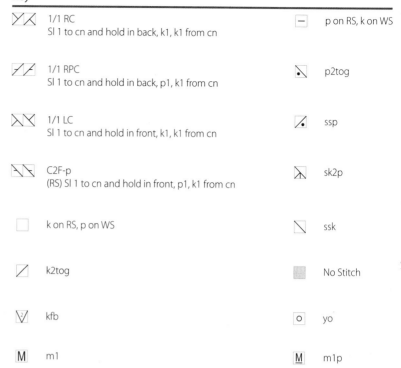

| | 1/1 RC |
| | Sl 1 to cn and hold in back, k1, k1 from cn |

| | 1/1 RPC |
| | Sl 1 to cn and hold in back, p1, k1 from cn |

| | 1/1 LC |
| | Sl 1 to cn and hold in front, k1, k1 from cn |

| | C2F-p |
| | (RS) Sl 1 to cn and hold in front, p1, k1 from cn |

| | k on RS, p on WS |

| | k2tog |

| | kfb |

| M | m1 |

| — | p on RS, k on WS |

| | p2tog |

| | ssp |

| | sk2p |

| | ssk |

| | No Stitch |

| o | yo |

| M | m1p |

Hem/Sleeve Lace Chart 2

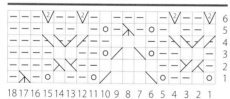

18 17 16 15 14 13 12 11 10 9 8 7 6 5 4 3 2 1

Next rnd: Knit and inc (dec, inc, dec) 2 (4, 6, 0) sts evenly around—48 (48, 64, 64) sts.

Work Hem Lace Chart 1—54 (54, 72, 72) sts.

Remove marker, k1, p1, replace marker. Work Hem Lace Chart 2.

BO in patt.

Finishing

Weave in ends. Block to finished measurements, smoothing garment flat in all directions, spreading lace flat at hems and cuffs, and firmly stretching/spreading hood in all directions.

Meme Shawl

One Hundred Years of Solitude

One Hundred Years of Solitude reads like one expansive, churning, dreamlike memory. And memory itself is a sort of magical realism: Time and events and details merge and jumble and reassemble into a fabricated memory, that—while seemingly perfectly lucid, perfectly certain—can be just as perfectly false. So it's no surprise that one of my favorite vignettes from the novel, and the initial inspiration for this shawl, was actually an artificial memory hodgepodged from three separate stories.

I very distinctly remembered Remedios the Beauty ascending through a hole in the bathroom roof after her bath, surrounded and carried off by a cloud of yellow butterflies. I was a little surprised to read it again and discover how wrong I'd gotten it.

It turns out I'd combined the rain of yellow flowers that blanketed Macondo after José Arcadio Buendía's death with the linen-sheeted ascension of Remedios the Beauty, and the butterflies that swarmed Mauricio Babilonia and later Meme, along with *both* Remedios' long hours spent in the bathroom with lovers or would-be lovers approaching on the roof, for good measure.

I've unraveled my misrememberance to produce an airy butterfly eyelet shawl. The filmy shawl uses weightless Malabrigo *Lace* and a design that is concentrated along the bottom edge, then disperses as it rises to the shoulders. If you want more freedom, skip the chart and place your butterflies at random, wherever you like.

SIZE
24" (61cm) × 68"(172.5cm)

MATERIALS
2 skeins Malabrigo *Lace* (100% baby merino wool, 470yd./430m per 1.75oz./50g). Shown in 22 Sauterne.

Weightless, übersoft fine Merino single.

US 6 (4mm) sharp needles (such as Addi lace, Knit Picks, etc.), 32" (80cm) length, *or size needed to obtain gauge*

GAUGE
20½ sts × 26 rows = 4" (10cm) in St st, blocked

Instructions

NOTES: The chart omits the sections of plain stockinette, which are indicated along the right-hand side noting the number of plain rows worked. Don't forget to maintain the garter edging on those rows.

The "butterflies" on Rows 57–60 are worked only every other repeat, and on Rows 61–64 every third repeat. You might find it helpful to place stitch markers at the beginning of the first repeat, then at the end of every repeat across the row.

CO 701 sts.

Row 1 (RS): Sl 1 wyib, [k2tog] across row—351 sts

Row 2 (WS): Sl 1 wyib, knit to end.

*Work Butterfly Chart, bottom.

Butterfly Chart, bottom

Butterfly Chart, top

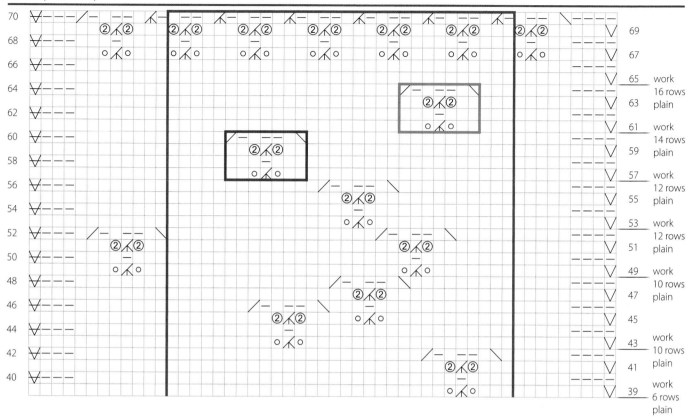

Key

☐	— k on RS, p on WS	②	— yo twice
−	— p on RS, k on WS	∨	— sl 1 wyib on RS
○	— yo	⩔	— sl 1 wyib on WS
╱	— k2tog on RS, p2tog on WS	☐	— Pattern repeat
╲	— ssk on RS, ssp on WS	■	— Work pattern every 3rd repeat; otherwise work these sts in St st
⋀	— k3tog on RS p3tog on WS	■	— Work pattern every 2nd repeat; otherwise work these sts in St st

Scarf Variation

Materials

2 skeins Malabrigo *Merino Worsted* (100% merino wool, 205yd./190m per 3.5 oz./100g).

US 9 (5.5mm) needles, *or size needed to obtain gauge*

Gauge

16 sts × 24 rows = 4" (10cm) in St st

NOTE: Only one 28-stitch repeat of the pattern will be worked between the edge stitches. Make sure to work the "butterflies" on Rows 57–60 and 61–64.

Loosely CO 51 sts.

Rows 1 & 2: Sl 1 wyib, knit to end.

Work shawl pattern from 1 to 65, including additional St st rows as noted, plus one more row in St st with garter edging. Then place sts on scrap yarn and set aside.

Make second half of scarf to match first, then join the two halves with Kitchener stitch (see instructions in the Epilogue).

Work 6 rows in St st, keeping 4 sts at beg and end of rows in garter st and slipping the first st of every row.

Work chart Rows 39–42. Continue with Butterfly Chart, top.

Work 10 rows in St st, keeping 4 sts at beg and end of rows in garter st and slipping the first st of every row.

Work chart Rows 43–48.

Work 10 rows in St st, keeping 4 sts at beg and end of rows in garter st and slipping the first st of every row.

Work chart Rows 49–52.

Work 12 rows in St st, keeping 4 sts at beg and end of rows in garter st and slipping the first st of every row.

Work chart Rows 53–56.

Work 12 rows in St st, keeping 4 sts at beg and end of rows in garter st and slipping the first st of every row.

Work chart Rows 57–60.

Work 14 rows in St st, keeping 4 sts at beg and end of rows in garter st and slipping the first st of every row.

Work chart Rows 61–64.

Work 16 rows in St st, keeping 4 sts at beg and end of rows in garter st and slipping the first st of every row.

Work chart Rows 65–70.*

Next 2 rows: Sl 1 wyib, knit to end.

BO as foll: Sl 1 wyib, [m1, pass first st over second st and off needle, k1, pass first st over second st and off needle] across row. Fasten off rem st.

Finishing

Weave in ends. Block to finished measurements.

Lucy Honeychurch Shawl

A Room with a View

I love Lucy Honeychurch. I love that she's "accomplished" but unpretentious, that she doubts herself, that she tries to stand up for what's right but can't always sort out what that is, that she plays with a passion she can't define or express away from the piano. I love her peevishness and I love her warmth and pluck and humor—though at this point, I can't separate the written Lucy from Helena Bonham Carter's performance of her (in what may be my very favorite movie adaptation of all time, probably because it's so like the book).

This warm Edwardian-inspired round shawl is the perfect wrap for winters at Windy Corner—or for your own romantic comedy, wherever it may be. It's knit in the round (read: all knitting, yay!) using Elizabeth Zimmerman's famous pi formula, and it's edged with a simple feather and fan pattern. Not only does it knit up very quickly, but the loose gauge also prevents the warm farmstead alpaca yarn from getting too heavy (important with a shawl worn folded in half) and the extra space really allows the airy halo to bloom. The whole circle is bound off then immediately picked up so that lace edge is more distinct and stable.

SIZE
43" (109cm) diameter

MATERIALS
4 skeins Alpacas of Wildcat Hollow *Sport* (100% alpaca, 200yd./183m per approx 3oz./85g). Shown in Carl (natural white, name varies by animal).

Soft twist 2-ply with lovely drape and stunning halo.

US 9 (5.5mm) double-pointed needles

US 9 circular needles, 32" (80cm) length, *or size needed to obtain gauge*

GAUGE
14 sts × 21 rows, unblocked (blocks to 12 sts × 21 rows) = 4" (10cm) in St st

Yo *pick up and k1 in bound-off edge, yo; rep from * around, picking up through the top loop only of each BO st—576 sts. Join for working in the rnd, pm for beg of rnd.

Knit 2 rnds.

Edging

Rnd 1: *(K2tog) 3 times, (yo, k1) 6 times, (k2tog) 3 times; rep from * around.

Rnds 2–4: Knit.

Rnds 5–8: Rep Rnds 1–4.

Rnd 9: Rep Rnd 1.

Rnds 10 and 12: Purl.

Rnd 11: Knit.

Rnd 13: Rep Rnd 1.

BO loosely kwise.

Finishing

Wet block to 43" (109cm) circumference.

Instructions

Using dpns, CO 9 sts.

Join for working in the rnd, pm for beg of rnd.

Rnd 1: Knit.

Rnd 2: *K1, m1; rep from * around—18 sts.

Rnds 3–5: Knit.

Rnd 6: *K1, m1; rep from * around—36 sts.

Rnds 7–12: Knit.

Rnd 13: *K1, m1; rep from * around—72 sts.

Rnds 14–25: Knit.

Rnd 26: *K1, m1; rep from * around—144 sts.

Rnds 27–50: Knit.

Rnd 51: *K1, m1; rep from * around—288 sts.

Rnds 52–91: Knit.

BO loosely but do not fasten off last st—1 st rem.

Jane Eyre Shawl

Jane Eyre

Although I admire the perfect balance of sense, will, and self-control Jane embodies as a woman, I love her but as a girl, in that first brave and injured outburst at the horrid Mrs. Reed. She is a pint-sized goddess of justice, champion of the wrongly accused, patron saint of the underdog. In her CraftLit podcast, Heather Underwood described *Jane Eyre* as something like "Wuthering Heights without the crazy," and that's about right. Despite its splashes of Gothic drama, it's an old-fashioned morality tale, where virtue is rewarded, and vice is punished.

A modest, natural gray with a striking lace feature, this warm shawl combines the quiet, no-nonsense style of the governess with the luxury of the heiress. Faroese shoulder shaping means it stays put; and the flame-pattered lace that spreads from the gusset gives a subtle nod to both the fire in Jane's spirit and the cleansing conflagration that finally changed her life forever.

SIZE
Women's One Size or Custom

MATERIALS
5 hanks Cascade *Eco Cloud* (70% undyed Merino/30% undyed baby alpaca; 164yd./150m per 3.5oz./100g). Shown in color 1810. (For custom-fit Foroese shaping on especially broad shoulders, add an extra skein.)

Airy knitted tube (essentially a 2-stitch I-cord) with Merino memory and alpaca drape, in natural, undyed colors.

US 9 (5.5mm) circular needles, 40" (100cm) length or longer (the longer, the better), and 2 double-pointed needles, *or size needed to obtain gauge*

US 7 (4.5mm) needles, any length, or size 7/G crochet hook

4 stitch markers of one color (M#1)

4 locking stitch markers of another color (M#2)

Cable needle

GAUGE
17 sts × 21 rows = 4" (10cm) in St st on larger needles

Pattern Notes

C2F: Sl 1 st to cn and hold in front, k1, k1 from cn.

C2B: Sl 1 st to cn and hold in back, k1, k1 from cn.

C3B: Sl 2 sts to cn and hold in back, k1, k2 from cn.

C3F: Sl 1 st to cn and hold in front, k2, k1 from cn.

Instructions

NOTES: [Brackets] mark off the back gusset, which has a little eyelet at the top, followed by a stockinette section, then flame lace. Eventually this section flares out and encloses the whole bottom border.

Flame lace is worked with lace pattern rows on both right and wrong sides of the shawl (it doesn't have an active front and a passive back like many lace patterns).

If you don't know how to cable without cable needles, now's the time to learn (see "Special Techniques" in the Epilogue). This pattern has a gazillion wee cables, perfect candidates for speedy cableless cabling!

Setup

With circular needles, CO 29 sts.

Row 1 (RS): Knit.

Row 2: P4, pm (M#1), k21, pm (M#1), p4.

Row 3: (C2F) twice, yo, m1, [(k2tog, yo) 10 times, k1], m1, yo, (C2B) twice—33 sts.

Row 4: P4, knit to last 4 sts, p4.

Row 5: (C2F) twice, yo, knit to marker, m1, [(k2tog, yo) 10 times, k1], m1, knit to last 4 sts, yo, (C2B) twice—37 sts.

Row 6: Purl to marker, knit to next marker, purl to end.

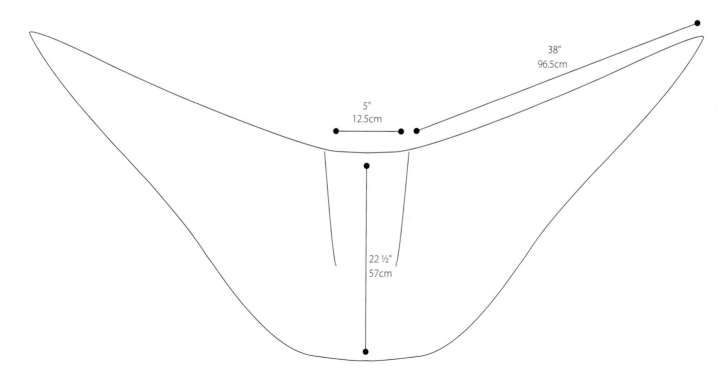

5"
12.5cm

38"
96.5cm

22 ½"
57cm

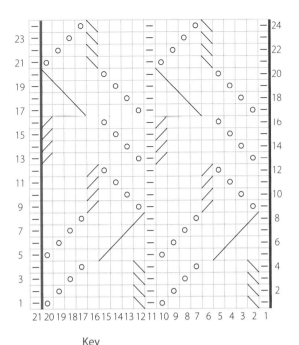

Key

☐	k on RS, p on WS
◿	k2tog on RS, p2tog on WS
—	p on RS, k on WS
◥	ssk on RS, ssp on WS
○	yo

Row 7: (C2F) twice, yo, k2, pm(M#2), knit to marker, m1, [k21], m1, k2, pm(M#2), knit to last 4 sts, yo, (C2B) twice—41 sts.

Row 8: Purl.

Shoulders

NOTE: You now have one shoulder marker (M#2) at each side and one marker (M#1) at each side of the gusset. You work every RS row of this section increasing with a yo just inside the cabled edging, increasing with a kfb on both sides of each shoulder marker, and increasing with a M1 just outside each side of the gusset—8 inc per RS row.

Row 1: (C2F) twice, yo, knit to 1 st before shoulder marker, kfb, sl m, kfb, knit to gusset marker, m1, sl m, [k21], sl m, m1, knit to 1 st before shoulder marker, kfb, sl m, kfb, knit to last 4 sts, yo, (C2B) twice—49 sts.

Row 2: Slipping markers as you come to them, purl.

Rep last 2 rows 15 more times, *or to desired size*—167 sts.

NOTE: If you have quite a small frame, check the fit after 10 or 12 repeats; for a larger frame, try it on after 16 repeats and see if you want to add more—but keep in mind that you'll need an extra skein.

Remove shoulder markers, leaving gusset markers in place.

Middle of Shawl and Gusset Lace

Gusset Lace Setup

Next row: (C2F) twice, yo, knit to gusset marker, m1, [k9, C3F, k9], m1, knit to last 4 sts, yo, (C2B) twice—171 sts.

While maintaining edge pattern and increases, and the increases at each side of the gusset, begin the Flame Lace Pattern across those 21 gusset stitches, starting from the WS.

Gusset Lace

Row 1: Purl to gusset marker, [work Row 1 of Flame Lace Pattern], purl to end.

Row 2: (C2F) twice, yo, knit to gusset marker, m1, [work Row 2 of Flame Lace Pattern], m1, knit to last 4 sts, yo, (C2B) twice—175 sts.

Rep the last 2 rows, working Flame Lace Pattern as established until 48 rows have been worked (2 full rep of Flame Lace Pattern)—271 sts.

Spreading Lace Pattern

Now comes the fun part! Move each gusset marker outward toward the edge by 10 stitches. Starting on the next row, your gusset pattern will have one extra repeat on each side (continue to work increases as in above rows: at each edge and just outside of the gusset on both sides).

After 4 rows, move each gusset marker out another 10 stitches and continue the pattern from where you left off. Continue in this way, moving the markers out every 4 rows, and maintaining the gusset and edge increases, working through the 23rd row (second to last) of the Flame Lace Pattern. At this point, your gusset area will be 141 stitches wide, and 319 stitches total.

Bottom of Shawl

Bottom Pattern Setup

Before working the final row of that repeat, count 70 sts out from each side's gusset marker and place a second marker.

NOTE: If you worked fewer or more than the 16 shoulder increases in these instructions, you may need to adjust this number up to 80 or down to 60. Either way, the markers must be at least 6 stitches from each end.

This is a setup row for the bottom edge lace, and adds nice pointy tips to the tops of your flames:

Next row: (C2F) twice, yo, knit to new marker, k9, (C3F, k7) 5 times, C3F, k8, remove gusset marker, [work Row 24 of Flame Lace Pattern], remove gusset marker, k8, (C3F, K7) 5 times, C3F, knit to last 4 sts, yo, (C2B) twice—321 sts.

Bottom Pattern

NOTE: You're still going to be increasing at the edge, but not right before/after the lace.

Row 1: Purl to marker, work Flame Lace Pattern to next marker, purl to end.

Row 2: (C2F) twice, yo, knit to marker work Flame Lace Pattern to next marker, knit to last 4 sts, yo, (C2B) twice—323 sts.

Work 22 more rows of Flame Lace Pattern and **at the same time,** after every 4 rows, move each marker out 10 sts as you did for the earlier flare; by the end, a full 24-row repeat of the Flame Lace Pattern has been worked—345 sts.

Bottom Edge

NOTE: This edging uses up darn near all of the yarn (I only had about 5 yards to spare). If you don't have quite enough, you can skip Row 2 below.

Row 1 (WS): Purl to marker, *k1, p9; rep from * to 1 st before marker, k1, purl to end.

Row 2: (C2F) twice, yo, k2tog, knit to marker, p1, *k9, p1; rep from * to marker, knit to last 6 sts, ssk, yo, (C2B) twice.

Rows 3 & 4: Sl 1, knit to marker, p1, *k2tog, yo, k2, p1, k2, yo, ssk, p1; rep from * to marker, knit to end.

BO loosely.

Neck Edge Reinforcement

NOTE: This reinforcement snugs up the neckline and stabilizes it to prevent stretching from the weight of the shawl. You can either crochet or knit the reinforcement; instructions for both options are provided.

Crochet: With crochet hook and RS facing, work a snug row of slip stitch along front and neck edges. Fasten off.

Knit: With dpns and RS facing, beg at lower-right front edge, snugly pick up and knit 2, *BO 1, pick up and knit 1; rep from * along front and neck edges. Fasten off rem st.

Finishing

Weave in ends. Soak, spin or press out water, and block flat, spreading lace flat and edges straight.

Lady Brett Ashley Pullover

The Sun Also Rises

E motional, clever, willful, selfish, and wild, Lady Brett Ashley epitomizes the conflicted flapper-era woman. Although she's not overly sympathetic, she does match the strength of the male characters, multiplied with sensuality, self-awareness, and an appealing, if somewhat doomed, perseverance and passion for living.

Brett's beauty and sex appeal are all the more striking against her boyish cropped hair and sometimes-masculine dress. This sporty pullover, inspired by the era's androgynous sportswear, although boxy, clings appealingly to curves. The flirty V-neck, seed stitch stripes, and middy-inspired tie give a nod to the patterns of the day, while the seamless, top-down construction is effortlessly modern.

SIZE
Women's S (M, L, XL)

MATERIALS
4 (4, 5, 6) skeins Stonehedge Fiber Mill *Shepherd's Wool* (100% fine wool, 250yd./229m per 4oz./113g). Shown in Blue Spruce.

A very smooth, classic worsted-spun 3-ply for crisp stitch definition, in heathers and solids.

US 8 (5mm) 32" (80cm) and 16" (40cm) circular needles, *or size needed to obtain gauge*

US 7 (4.5mm) 32" (80cm) circular needles

GAUGE
18 sts × 26 rows = 4" (10cm) over St st and Seed St on larger needles

Pattern Notes

Seed Stitch

(multiple of 2 sts)

Row 1: *K1, p1; rep from * to end.

Row 2: Purl the knit sts and knit the purl sts.

Rep Rows 1 and 2 for patt.

Instructions

Yoke

With larger 32" (80cm) circular needle, CO 4 (4, 6, 6), pm, CO 14 (14, 16, 16), pm, CO 26 (26, 28, 28), pm, CO 14 (14, 16, 16), pm, CO 4 (4, 6, 6)—62 (62, 72, 72) sts.

Row 1 (RS): Sl 1, *knit to 1 st before marker, (kfb) twice; rep from * 3 more times, knit to end—8 sts increased.

Rows 2, 4 and 6: Sl 1, purl to last st, k1.

Row 3: Rep Row 1—8 sts increased.

Row 5: Sl 1, kfb, *knit to 1 st before marker, (kfb) twice; rep from * 3 more times, knit to last 2 sts, kfb, k1—10 sts increased.

Rows 7–24: Rep Rows 1–6 three more times—88 (88, 98, 98) sts.

Row 25: Sl 1, k2 *(k1, p1) to 1 st before marker, (kfb) twice; rep from * 3 more times, (k1, p1) to last 3 sts, k3—8 sts increased.

Rows 26, 28, 30, 32, 34 and 36: Sl 1, p2, *work in Seed St to 2 sts before marker, p4; rep from * 3 more times, work in Seed St to last 3 sts, p2, k1.

Row 27: Sl 1, k2, *work in Seed St to 1 st before marker, (kfb) twice; rep from * 3 more times, work in Seed St to last 3 sts, k3—8 sts increased.

Row 29: Sl 1, kfb, *work in Seed St to 1 st before marker, (kfb) twice; rep from 3 more times, work in Seed St to last 3 sts, kfb, k2—10 sts increased.

Rows 31 and 33: Rep Row 27—8 sts increased.

Row 35: Rep Row 29—218 (218, 228, 228) sts.

Rep Rows 1–6 0 (1, 2, 3) time(s), Rows 5 and 6 twice more, then Row 5 once more—248 (274, 310, 336) sts. Piece measures about 6¼ (7¼, 8¼, 9)" (16 [18.5, 21, 23]cm) from CO edge. Do not turn at end of last row.

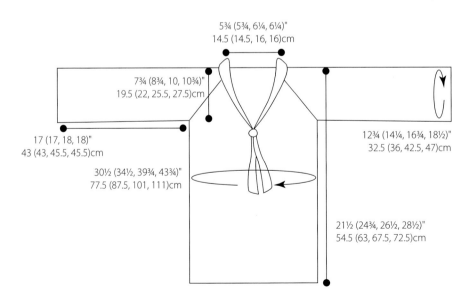

5¾ (5¾, 6¼, 6¼)"
14.5 (14.5, 16, 16)cm

7¾ (8¾, 10, 10¾)"
19.5 (22, 25.5, 27.5)cm

17 (17, 18, 18)"
43 (43, 45.5, 45.5)cm

12¾ (14¼, 16¾, 18½)"
32.5 (36, 42.5, 47)cm

30½ (34½, 39¾, 43¾)"
77.5 (87.5, 101, 111)cm

21½ (24¾, 26½, 28½)"
54.5 (63, 67.5, 72.5)cm

Divide for Sleeves

With RS still facing and removing markers as you get to them, CO 1, join for working in the rnd, and knit across to the first marker, place 56 (62, 70, 76) sleeve sts on waste yarn or spare circular needle. CO 0 (1, 2, 3) sts, pm, CO 0 (1, 2, 3) sts, knit across 68 (74, 82, 88) back sts, place 56 (62, 70, 76) sleeve sts on waste yarn or spare circular needle, CO 0 (1, 2, 3) sts, pm, CO 0 (1, 2, 3) sts, and knit across front sts and up to first marker—137 (155, 179, 197) sts.

Knit 6 (4, 0, 0) rnds even.

Work 10 rnds in Seed St; the odd number of sts prevents 2 knit or 2 purl stitches falling next to each other at the beginning/end of rounds.

Knit 12 (16, 18, 20) rnds.

Work 8 rnds in Seed St.

Knit 12 (16, 18, 20) rnds.

Work 6 rnds in Seed St.

Knit 12 (16, 18, 20) rnds.

Work 4 rnds in Seed St.

Knit 12 (16, 18, 20) rnds.

Work 8 rnds in Seed St. Piece should measure about 13¾ (16, 16½, 17¾)" (35 [40.5, 42, 45] cm) from bottom of armholes.

BO in pattern.

Sleeves

Place 56 (62, 70, 76) sleeve sts on 16" (40 cm) needle. With RS facing, pick up and k1 st over gap, 1 (3, 5, 7) over CO sts, then1 st over other gap—59 (67, 77, 85) sts.

Size S only: Knit across sleeve sts to first st picked up in gap, sl 1, k2tog, psso—57 sts.

Sizes M (L, XL) only: Knit across sleeve sts to first st picked up in gap, ssk (first gap st and first underarm st), k1 (3, 5), k2tog (last underarm st and second gap st)—65 (75, 83) sts.

All sizes: Continue in St st until sleeve measures 13¼ (12¾, 13½, 13)" (33.5 [32.5, 34.5, 33] cm) from bottom of armhole.

Work 4 rnds in Seed St.

Knit 12 (16, 18, 20) rnds.

Work 8 rnds in Seed St. Sleeve should measure about 17 (17, 18, 18)" (43, 43, 45.5, 45.5] cm) from bottom of armhole.

BO in pattern.

Repeat with other sleeve.

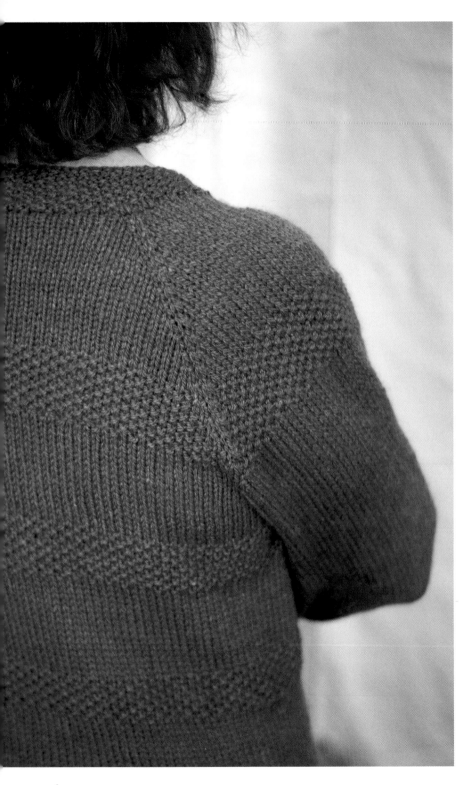

Collar

With smaller 32" (80 cm) needle, CO 75 (80, 85, 90) sts. Starting at center of V with RS facing, pick up and k1 st for each slipped st on right side of neck, 1 st for each CO st along top of sleeves and back neck, and 1 st for each slipped st on left side of neck, then CO 75 (80, 85, 90) more sts—254 (270, 296, 312) sts.

Rows 1–10: Sl 1, kfb, work in Seed St to last st, k1—264 (280, 306, 322) sts.

BO In pattern.

Finishing

Weave in ends. Block to finished measurements. Tie collar tails to wear.

Anne Shirley Puff-Sleeve Top

Anne of Green Gables

With her earnest manner and vivid imagination, Anne represents the full flowering of youthful creativity blossoming in a plain, gray setting. As an orphan who remains true to herself and thrives and enriches everyone around her, Anne is the perfect model for any child who feels like a lonely, weird outsider. In a quiet, no-nonsense household, she's always grateful for her adopted home, but longs for the frills and puffs of the other girls.

This sweater was inspired by the dress that the quiet but observant Matthew gave Anne for Christmas, which was Anne's first taste of extravagance after a life of serviceable but "skimpy" garments. It's worked in a rich auburn color, a tribute to the beloved redhead, and, like Anne's treasured dress, this sweater has two rows of the much-coveted puffs at the sleeves. Leave it plain for a modern look; or, if you like frills, deck the sleeves with brown silk ribbons (the rapid puff decreases form little gaps, perfect for threading ribbon), just like Anne's cherished dress.

SIZE
Women's S (M, L, XL)

MATERIALS
6 (6, 7, 7) hanks Quince & Co. *Lark* (100% American Wool, 134yd./123m per 1.75oz./50g). Shown in Gingerbread.

Plump, lofty, soft wool 4-ply worsted.

US 5 (3.75mm) 24" (60cm) circulars or dpns, 2 circulars, or long circular for Magic Loop

US 7 (4.5mm) 24" (60cm) circulars + dpns, 2 circulars, or long circular for Magic Loop, *or size needed to obtain gauge*

Stitch markers in 2 colors or types

Scrap yarn to hold sleeve stitches

2 yd. (1.75m) 1¼" (3cm) wide ribbon (optional)

GAUGE
17½ sts & 26 rows = 4" (10cm) in St st on larger needles

Instructions

NOTE: This garment is quite stretchy and designed to be close fitting. Each size can nicely accommodate a bustline several inches larger than the schematic.

Neckband

With smaller needles, CO 100 sts. Join for working in the rnd, pm for beg of rnd.

Work 1¾ (2, 2¼, 2½)" (4.5 [5, 5.5, 6.5]cm) in k1, p1 ribbing.

Set Up Rows for Raglan Increases

Change to larger needles. Using the same type of markers as the beg of rnd marker; k16, pm, k34, pm, k16, pm, knit to end.

Shoulders

Raglan Increases

Row 1: *Kfb, knit to 1 st before raglan marker, kfb; rep from * 3 more times—8 sts increased.

Row 2: Knit.

Rep last 2 rnds 2 (3, 4, 5) more times—124 (132, 140, 148) sts.

Make First Puff

NOTE: Use the second type of markers here.

Row 1: *Kfb, k5 (6, 7, 8), pm, (kfb) 10 times, pm, knit to 1 st before raglan marker, (kfb) twice, knit to 1 st before raglan marker, kfb; rep from * once more—28 sts increased (10 per sleeve, 8 raglan).

Row 2: *K7 (8, 9, 10), (kfb) 20 times*, knit to raglan marker before 2nd sleeve; rep from * to * once more, then knit to end—40 sts increased (20 per sleeve).

Rep Rows 1 and 2 of Raglan Increases 4 (5, 6, 7) more times, being careful not to accidentally increase around puff markers—224 (240, 256, 272) sts.

Decrease First Puff

Rows 1 & 3: *Kfb, knit to puff marker, (k2tog tbl) to next puff marker, knit to 1 st before raglan marker, (kfb) twice, knit to 1 st before raglan marker, kfb; rep from * once more—180 (196, 212, 228) sts.

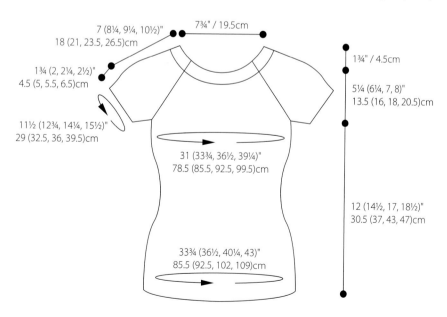

7 (8¼, 9¼, 10½)"
18 (21, 23.5, 26.5)cm

7¾" / 19.5cm

1¾ (2, 2¼, 2½)"
4.5 (5, 5.5, 6.5)cm

1¾" / 4.5cm

5¼ (6¼, 7, 8)"
13.5 (16, 18, 20.5)cm

11½ (12¾, 14¼, 15½)"
29 (32.5, 36, 39.5)cm

31 (33¾, 36½, 39¼)"
78.5 (85.5, 92.5, 99.5)cm

12 (14½, 17, 18½)"
30.5 (37, 43, 47)cm

33¾ (36½, 40¼, 43)"
85.5 (92.5, 102, 109)cm

Rep Rows 1 and 2 of Raglan Increases 4 (5, 6, 7) more times, being careful not to accidentally increase around puff markers—280 (304, 328, 352) sts.

Decrease Second Puff

Work as described in the earlier "Decrease First Puff" section—236 (260, 284, 308) sts.

Divide for sleeves

Place 50 (56, 62, 68) sleeve sts on scrap yarn; knit 68 (74, 80, 86) back sts, leaving one marker at side; rep for other sleeve and front—136 (148, 160, 172) sts.

Bust

Work even in St st for 2 (3, 4, 4½)" (5 [7.5, 10, 11.5]cm) from armpit, or to cover your bust (transfer half the sts to a spare needle to try it on). If your breasts are large for your size, you can work several short rows on one side only of this section.

Waist

Change to smaller needles and work 3 (3½, 4, 4½)" (7.5 [9, 10, 11.5]cm) in k1, p1 ribbing.

Hip

Change to larger needles. kfb, knit to 1 st before side marker, (kfb) twice, knit to 1 st before end of rnd marker, kfb—4 sts increased.

Continue in St st and rep inc every 12th rnd 2 (2, 3, 3) times—148 (160, 176, 188) sts.

Work even in St st until piece measures 5 (5½, 6, 6½)" (12.5 [14, 15, 16.5]cm) from waist rib.

With same (larger) needles, work 2 (2½, 3, 3)" (5 [6.5, 7.5, 7.5]cm) in k1, p1 ribbing. BO in pattern.

Rows 2 & 4: Knit to puff marker, kbl to next puff marker, knit to next puff marker, kbl to next puff marker, knit to end.

Make Second Puff

Row 1: *Kfb, knit to puff marker, (kfb) 10 times, knit to 1 st before raglan marker, (kfb) twice, knit to 1 st before raglan marker, kfb*; rep from * once more—28 sts increased. (20 per sleeve, 8 raglan)

Row 2: *Knit to puff marker, (kfb) 20 times*, knit to raglan marker before 2nd sleeve; rep from * to * once more, then knit to end—40 sts increased. (20 per sleeve, 8 raglan)

Sleeves

Place 50 (56, 62, 68) held sleeve sts on smaller dpns. Pick up and k2 sts over gap at bottom of armhole and pm for rnd between 2 picked up sts—52 (58, 64, 70) sts.

Rnd 1: K2tog, knit to last 2 sts, ssk—50 (56, 62, 68) sts.

Work 1¾ (2, 2¼, 2½)" (4.5 [5, 5.5, 6.5]cm) in k1, p1 ribbing. BO in pattern.

Repeat for other sleeve.

Finishing

Weave in ends. Block to finished measurements.

If using ribbon in sleeves, cut ribbon into 4 pieces. Using a blunt yarn needle, thread a piece of ribbon through sleeve at first ruffle decrease/second ruffle increase. Fold ribbon about 4" (10cm) from one end, loop folded end around a finger and pull folded end through loop and tighten, adjusting the knot. Repeat on other end of ribbon, gathering sleeve along ribbon to further puff sleeve. Thread a second ribbon through sleeve at second ruffle decrease and knot ends. Repeat for other sleeve.

3

In Which We Knit

for Men

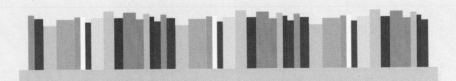

Ishmael Sweater

Moby Dick

I don't know why *Moby Dick* gets such a bad rap. *Moby Dick* is a hoot, thanks to the book's sometimes cheeky, sometimes melodramatic, but always amusing and long-winded narrator, Ishmael. From his comical descriptions of sharing a bunk with Quequeg to his spot-on mimicry of the sundry iconic characters aboard ship to his absurdly encyclopedic explanations of *every*thing, Ishmael keeps the dark and primal tale unexpectedly light (though, admittedly, incredibly long).

For Ishmael, rather a bit too urbane and sophisticated for a seaman: a modern response to the classic fisherman's sweater. Instead of scratchy gray fisherman's wool, this sweater is worked in wonderfully soft superwash Merino in rich, kettle-dyed colors. But some practical details remain: a high cushiony collar to keep out the cold and long cuffs that let the full-length sleeves quickly convert to the classic fisherman's ⅞ length, which keeps the sleeves clean and dry when he needs to get his hands dirty.

SIZE

Men's S (M, L, XL)

MATERIALS

8 (9, 10, 11) skeins Malabrigo *Rios* (100% superwash wool; 210 yd./192 m per 3.5oz./100g). Shown in 869 Cumparsita.

A smooth, plied superwash merino in rich kettle-dyed hues.

US 7 (4.5mm) circular needles, 16" (40cm) *and* 32" (80cm) lengths, *or size needed to obtain gauge*

US 5 (3.75mm) pointy circular needles, 16" (40cm) *and* 32" (80cm) lengths

8 stitch markers (ideally, 2 different colors)

4 locking stitch markers

Cable needle or wood/bamboo double-pointed needle

GAUGE

19 sts × 26 rows = 4" (10cm) in St st on larger needles

Instructions

NOTE: Several of the Rios colorways are noted for variations that can be very different from skein to skein, even within the same dye lot. If you're using one of those colorways (Cumparsita is one), you might want to alternate between 2 balls throughout to maintain better overall color harmony. You should also set aside the 2 most similar skeins for the sleeves before you get started.

Turtleneck

With smaller needles, CO 116 (116, 132, 132). Join for working in the rnd, pm for beg of rnd.

Work 7" (18cm) in k2, p2 ribbing.

Decreasing BO/Increasing Pick Up to Stabilize Collar

BO as follows: *k2, p2tog; rep from * around—do not fasten off last st. Without cutting yarn or turning work, pick up and k86 (86, 98, 98) sts along BO edge—87 (87, 99, 99) sts. Join for working in the rnd, pm for beg of rnd.

Next rnd: *K2, kfb; rep from * around—116 (116, 132, 132) sts.

Change to larger needles.

S/M Sleeve Chart

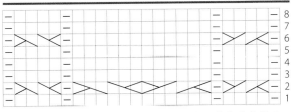

L/XL Sleeve Chart

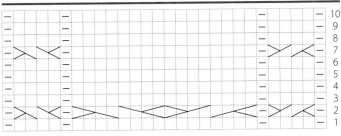

S/M Front Chart

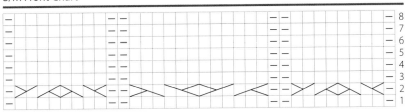

L/XL Front Chart

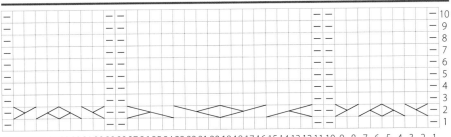

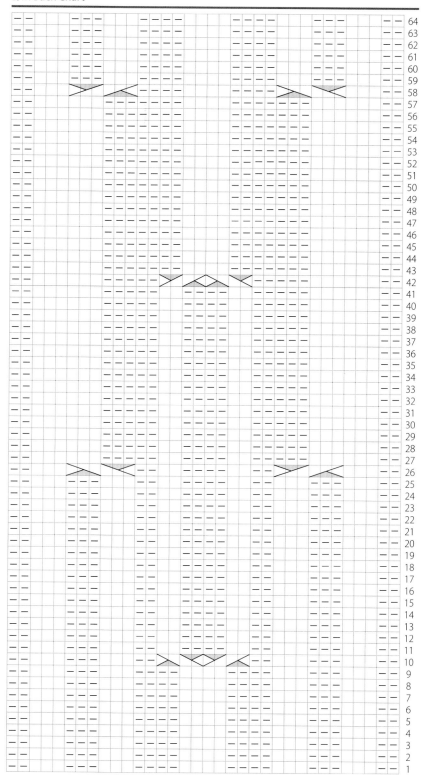

Yoke

NOTE: Normally, I don't bother with the mirrored versions of m1, but in this case it really does make a difference, so use the specified one.

Yoke Setup

Rnd 1: Working charts for your size, work Sleeve Chart over first 24 (24, 28, 28) sts, pm, Front Chart over next 34 (34, 38, 38) sts, pm, Sleeve Chart over next 24 (24, 28, 28) sts, pm, then Back Chart over rem 34 (34, 38, 38) sts.

Rnd 2: Work sleeve chart, sm, m1r, pm, work Front Chart, sm, m1l, pm, work Sleeve Chart, sm, m1r, pm, work Back Chart, sm, m1l, pm for new end of rnd marker—120 (120, 136, 136) sts.

Rnd 3: Work Sleeve Chart, sm, k1, m1l, sm, work Front Chart, sm, m1r, k1, sm, work Sleeve Chart, sm, k1, m1l, sm, work Back Chart, sm, m1r, k—124 (124, 140, 140) sts.

Rest of Yoke

Continue to work the charts, and increase on both sides of plain stockinette sections (*not* both sides of markers) every other rnd. On the inc rnds, you use a m1r just after each pattern section (beginning of each stockinette section) and a m1l at the end of each stockinette section (just before each pattern section).

Rnd 4 and all other even-numbered rnds: Work Sleeve Chart, sm, m1r, knit to marker, m1l, sm, work Front Chart, sm, m1r, knit to marker, m1l, sm, work Sleeve Chart, sm, m1r, knit to marker, m1l, sm, work Back Chart, sm, m1r, knit to end, m1l—8 sts increased each rnd.

Rnd 5 and all other odd-numbered rnds: Work charts and knit St st sections as established, working new sts in St st.

Rep last 2 rnds 24 (28, 30, 35) more times, then work 3 (3, 5, 5) rnds even; you should have 7 (8, 7, 8) full repeats of the Sleeve Charts—324 (356, 388, 428) sts.

Tips:

- Using 1 color marker before each charted section and a 2nd color after each charted section can remind you where and what type of increases you're working.

- Cables on the Back Chart only occur every other set, on the same row as the other major cables.

- It's a good idea to count your stockinette section sts every odd row so you catch it right away if you've neglected an increase. After the initial setup section, your count should always be an even number.

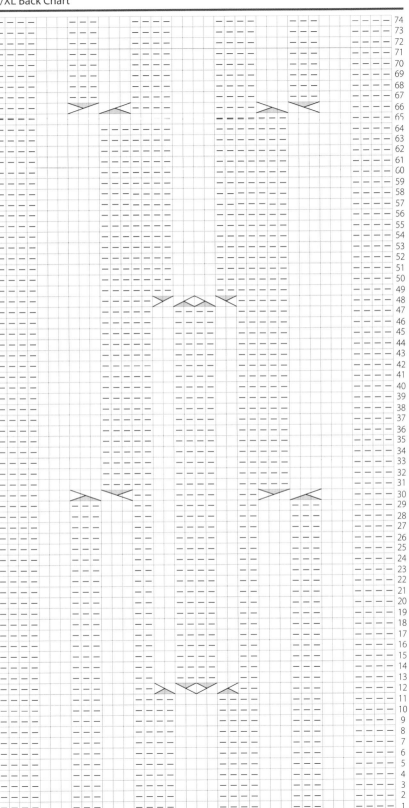

k

— p

2/2 LC
Sl 2 to cn and hold in front, k2, k2 sts from cn

2/2 RC
Sl 2 to cn and hold in back, k2, k2 sts from cn

3/3 LC
Sl 3 to cn and hold in front, k3, k3 sts from cn

3/3 RC
Sl 3 to cn and hold in back, k3, k3 sts from cn

4/4 RC
Sl 4 to cn and hold in back, k4, k4 sts from cn

4/4 LC
Sl 4 to cn and hold in front, k4, k4 sts from cn

2/2 LPC
Sl 2 to cn, hold to front, p2, k2 from cn

2/2 RPC
Sl 2 to cn, hold to back, k2, p2 from cn

3/3 RPC
Sl 3 to cn and hold in back, k3, p3 sts from cn

3/3 LPC
Sl 3 to cn and hold in front, p3, k3 sts from cn

Divide for Sleeves

Use your locking stitch markers to mark the middle of each stockinette section, then move each one 4 (8, 8, 12) sts toward sleeve panel. This adds a bit more area to the front and back—94 (110, 118, 136) sts each for front and back, and 68 (68, 76, 78) sts for each sleeve.

To get to your new round starting point, work in pattern to your first locking marker. This is your new start of rnd.

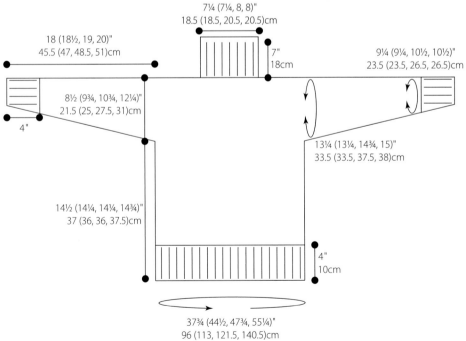

7¼ (7¼, 8, 8)"
18.5 (18.5, 20.5, 20.5)cm

7"
18cm

18 (18½, 19, 20)"
45.5 (47, 48.5, 51)cm

9¼ (9¼, 10½, 10½)"
23.5 (23.5, 26.5, 26.5)cm

8½ (9¾, 10¾, 12¼)"
21.5 (25, 27.5, 31)cm

4"

13¼ (13¼, 14¾, 15)"
33.5 (33.5, 37.5, 38)cm

14½ (14¼, 14¼, 14¾)"
37 (36, 36, 37.5)cm

4"
10cm

37¾ (44½, 47¾, 55¼)"
96 (113, 121.5, 140.5)cm

To divide, work in patt across front to next locking marker, place next 68 (68, 76, 78) sleeve sts on scrap yarn, work across back sts in patt to next locking marker, place next 68 (68, 76, 78) sleeve sts on scrap yarn—188 (220, 236, 272) sts rem. Join for working in the rnd, leaving one locking marker in place on side of body. This was Rnd 1 of your next repeat.

Continue to work charts and knit St st sections even.

Continue even in established patt until sweater, measured along center of back from just below collar, measures 19 (20, 21, 23)" (48.5 [51, 53.5, 58.5]cm).

Change to smaller needles. Work 4" (10cm) in k2, p2 ribbing. BO in patt.

Sleeves

Right Sleeve: Place 68 (68, 76, 78) sleeve sts on larger 16" (40cm) circular needles. With RS facing, join yarn and pick up and k4 sts at the bottom of the armhole—72 (72, 80, 82) sts.

Work across sleeve, maintaining patt (remember you already worked Rnd 1 on the right sleeve when you divided for sleeves) to last sleeve st before picked up sts, ssk the last sleeve st together with the first picked up st, k1, pm, k1, k2tog the last picked up st and first sleeve st—70 (70, 78, 80) sts. New marker indicates beg of rnd.

Continue in established patt and dec 1 st on each side of beg of rnd marker every 10th row 9 (9, 9, 10) times with ssk at beg of rnd and k2tog at end of rnd—52 (52, 60, 60) sts.

Work even until sleeve measures 14 (14½, 15, 16)" (35.5 [37, 38, 40.5]cm) from underarm.

Change to smaller needles. Work 4" (10cm) in k2, p2 ribbing. BO in patt.

Left Sleeve: Place 68 (68, 76, 78) sleeve sts on larger 16" (40cm) circular needles. With RS facing, join yarn

and work Rnd 1 pattern across sleeve, pick up and k4 sts at the bottom of the armhole—72 (72, 80, 82) sts.

Continue as for Right Sleeve, proceeding with Rnd 2 of pattern.

Finishing

Weave in ends. Block to finished measurements.

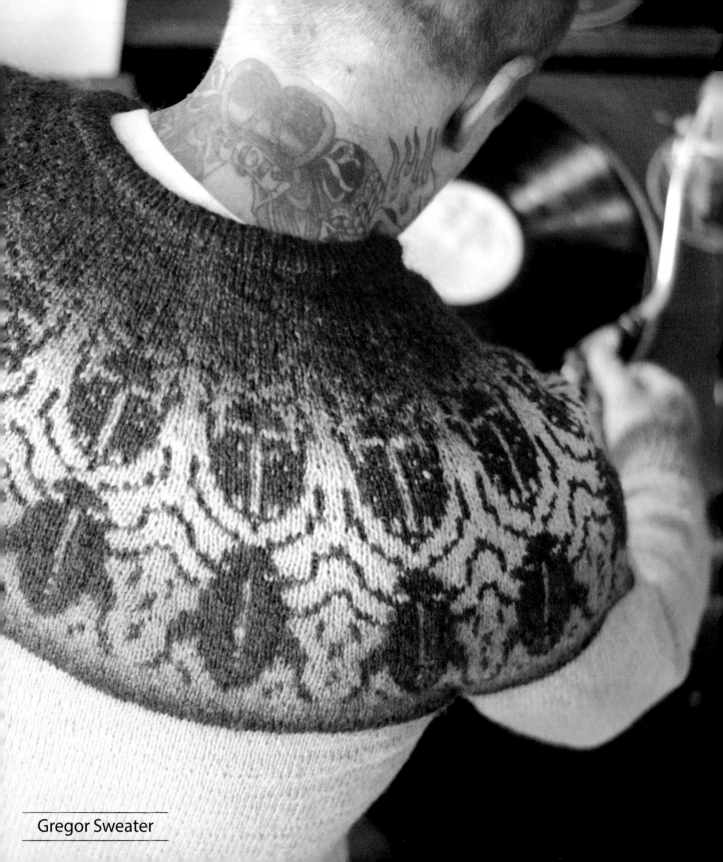

Gregor Sweater

Gregor Sweater

The Metamorphosis

Inspired by the Gregor Samsa's hideous existential predicament, this sweater, infested with creepy-crawlies, is both mezmerizing and a bit off-putting. The bug pattern itself transitions from an almost cute stylized bug to a horrible thing with meaty legs and wriggling antennae. At the same time, the background yarn, with its long repeats, softly changes colors.

SIZE
Men's S (M, L, XL)

MATERIALS
Yoke Background Color (YC): 2 balls Kauni Wool *8/2 Effektgarn* (100% wool; 665 yd./600m per 5.3oz./150g). Shown in Color EV.

A toothy plied wool with ultra-long color progressions (fewer than two full repeats per 150g).

Yoke Contrast Color (CC): 1 skein Harrisville Designs *New England Shetland* (100% wool; 217yd./198m per 1.75oz./50g). Shown in Color 38 teak.

A classic toothy Shetland wool with rich heathered solids.

Main Color (MC): 2 (2, 3, 3) balls Kauni Wool *8/2 Solids* (100% wool; 665 yd./600m per 5.3oz./150g). Shown in Color RR1.

A toothy classic plied fingering wool in solids and heathered solids.

US 0 (2mm) 16" (40cm) circular needles, dpns, or longer circular needle for Magic Loop

US 1 (2.25mm) 16" (40cm) and 32" (80cm) needles, or 40" (100cm) circular needles, *or size needed to obtain gauge*

US 1.5 (2.5mm) 16" (40cm) and 32" (80cm) needles, or 40" (100cm) circular needles (this is optional for the colorwork portion of the yoke; use the larger needle size to keep your colorwork from getting too tight)

Scrap yarn

GAUGE

26 sts × 39 rows = 4" (10cm) in St st on size US 1 (2.25mm) needles

Instructions

Yarn Setup

If you're using the EV color for your YC, unwind the ball so you're starting the red a bit before it transitions to yellow. If you're using a different color, make sure your YC doesn't have any colors in the progression or transitions that are too close to CC. You'll use about ⅔ of the ball, so you might be able to work around a close color. I recommend rewinding the ball so you can see the colors inside and be sure you're safe. It's worth the effort to avoid frogging 6" (15cm) of colorwork. Not that I did that. Ahem.

Collar

With smallest needles and YC, CO 144. Join for working in the rnd, pm for beg of rnd.

Rnds 1–6: *K1, p1, rep from * to end.

Rnd 7: Knit.

Yoke

NOTE: If you knit colorwork two-handed, hold the YC in your right hand (English) and the CC in your left hand (continental).

Change to larger needles (or largest size, if your colorwork tends to be tight).

NOTE: Pm between each rep on the first rnd to keep your work orderly.

Rnds 1–70: Join CC and work entire colorwork chart—400 sts.

(If your colorwork tends to be tight, you might switch back to smaller needles for Rnd 9, then change back to the larger needle when beginning Rnd 10.)

After completing the pattern, change to the medium-size needles if you were using the largest ones. Cut CC and continue in YC.

Knit 1 (8, 1, 1) rnd(s).

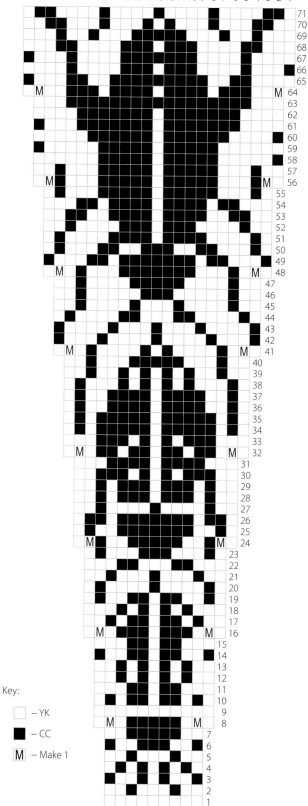

Key:
- □ – YK
- ■ – CC
- M – Make 1

Sizes S and M only:

Change to MC and go to the "Divide for Sleeves" section.

Sizes L and XL only:

Next rnd: K5, *m1, k15, m1, k10; rep from * 14 more times, m1, k15, m1, k5—432 (432) sts.

Knit 8 rnds even. Change to MC.

Size L only:

Go to the "Divide for Sleeves" section.

Size XL only:

Next rnd: K6, *m1, k15, m1, k12; rep from * 14 more times, m1, k15, m1, k6—464 sts.

Knit 8 rnds even.

Measure two pieces of YC from the second ball to match the color at the yoke, each about 10 yds (9m) long, and set it aside for the sleeve cuffs.

Divide for Sleeves

Next rnd: *Knit 125 (125, 135, 145) sts and remove first 4 end-of-rep markers (5 rep), place next 75 (75, 81, 87) sts (3 rep) on waste yarn for sleeve, CO 10 (20, 10, 10) sts, pm; rep from * once more—270 (290, 290, 310) sts, with 4 gusset markers.

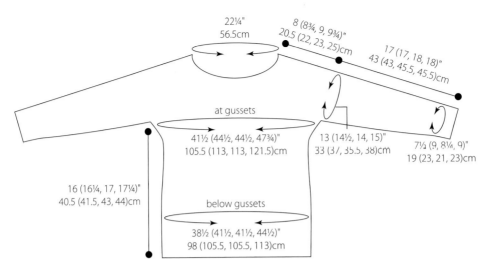

22¼"
56.5cm

8 (8¾, 9, 9¾)"
20.5 (22, 23, 25)cm

17 (17, 18, 18)"
43 (43, 45.5, 45.5)cm

at gussets

41½ (44½, 44½, 47¾)"
105.5 (113, 113, 121.5)cm

13 (14½, 14, 15)"
33 (37, 35.5, 38)cm

7¼ (9, 8¼, 9)"
19 (23, 21, 23)cm

16 (16¼, 17, 17¼)"
40.5 (41.5, 43, 44)cm

below gussets

38½ (41½, 41½, 44½)"
98 (105.5, 105.5, 113)cm

Gusset

Knit 1 rnd.

Next rnd: Knit to m, ssk, knit to 2 sts before next m, k2tog; rep from * once more—4 sts dec'd.

Rep last 2 rnds 4 more times—250 (270, 270, 290) sts.

NOTE: On sizes S (L, XL) only, the underarm gusset forms a V; on size M, the decrease lines taper but do not meet at the bottom of the gussets.

Body

Continue in St st until piece measures 22 (23, 24, 25)" (56 [58.5, 61, 63.5] cm), or 2" (5cm) less than final desired length along center of body from CO edge.

Change to smallest circular needle and YC. Work k1, p1 ribbing for 2" (5cm). BO in patt.

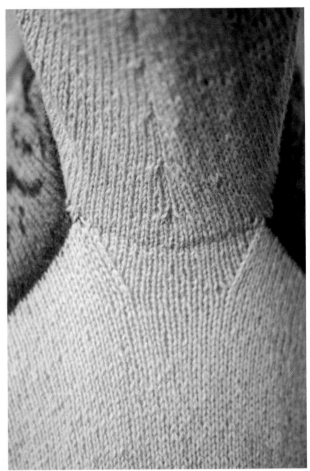

Underarm gusset; gussets on all other sides meet at center

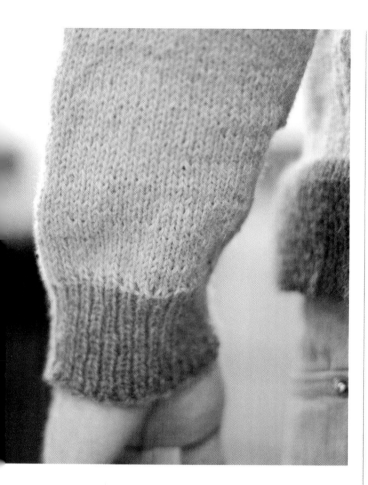

Change to smallest needles and reserved YC.

Next rnd: *K1, p1; rep from * to last 3 sts, k2tog, p1—48 (58, 52, 58) sts.

Work 2" (5cm) in k1, p1 ribbing. BO in patt.

Rep for other sleeve.

Finishing

Weave in ends. Block to finished measurements.

Sleeves

Place 75 (75, 81, 87) sleeve sts on larger 16" (40cm) needle or longer circular needle for Magic Loop, pick up and k2 sts at the gap, 10 (20, 10, 10) sts along underarm CO edge, then 2 sts at gap—85 (95, 91, 97) sts.

Next rnd: Knit, pm at center underarm for beg of rnd.

Continue in St st and **at the same time,** dec every 8th rnd 18 (18, 19, 19) times as follows: k2tog, knit to last 2 sts, ssk—49 (59, 53, 59) sts rem when dec are complete. Work even until sleeve measures 15 (15, 16, 16)" (38 [38, 40.5, 40.5]cm) from armpit, or 2" (5cm) less than desired length.

Sal Paradise Vest

On the Road

I think of *On the Road* as sort of a *Catcher in the Rye* for loveable reprobates. It's still an anthem for (albeit somewhat older) dropouts and misfits, but without all the whining, and with way more debauched fun. It gets that youthful sense of having all the time in the world, but still wanting to cram it with wild adventure in wide-open spaces. Although everyone loves to watch a charismatic lunatic like Dean Moriarty, like most people, I can better relate to Sal.

Inspired by the laid-back Beat style, this vest updates a simple '50s design with seamless modern construction, making this classic vest as easy to knit as it is to wear. The lightweight wool-blend yarn has a gentle halo and a subdued color progression that gives it an instant faded vintage look.

The vest is cast on over waste yarn at center back. It's knit flat, from the back up over the shoulders down to the center front where it's shaped into a V. Then it's all joined up in the round and knit straight down to the hem.

SIZES
Men's S (M, L, XL)

MATERIALS
5 (6, 6, 7) balls Valley Yarns *Cold Spring* (39% wool/36% fine acrylic/25% baby alpaca, 108yd./99m per 1.75oz./50g). Shown in 06 Forest Canopy.

Lofty, fuzzy aran weight wool blend with very long, very subtle color progressions.

US 7 (4.5mm) circular needles, 24" (60cm) length, *or size needed to obtain gauge*

US 5 (3.75mm) circular needles, 16" (40cm) and 24" (60cm) length

Waste yarn of the same gauge

Stitch holder

GAUGE
17 sts × 24 rnds = 4" (10cm) in St st with larger needles

Instructions

NOTE: For all flat rows, you should *always slip the first stitch purlwise and knit the last st of every row*, regardless of whether it's explicitly stated in the instructions. So if the Instructions just say to purl the row, you still slip that first stitch and knit the last stitch. (No kittens will die if you forget to do this, but it does make picking up the edging a bigger pain.)

Back Yoke

With larger needles, CO 60 (70, 80, 90) sts with waste yarn. Join project yarn.

Row 1 (RS): Knit.

Row 2: Purl.

Armhole Shaping

Row 3 (dec): Sl 1, k2, ssk, knit to last 5 sts, k2tog, k3—58 (68, 78, 88) sts.

Work 1 row even in St st. Rep Row 3 on next RS row, then every 4th row (every other RS row) 4 (4, 5, 5) more times—48 (58, 66, 76) sts rem.

Center Back

Work 17 (19, 21, 25) rows even in St st, ending with a WS row.

Back Neck Bind Off and Shaping

Next row (RS): Sl 1, k11 (11, 13, 15), k2tog, k1 (right shoulder), BO 18 (28, 32, 32) sts for neck, 14 (14, 16, 18) sts remain on left needle, and 1 st on right needle after last bound off st, k1, ssk, knit to end (left shoulder)—14 (14, 16, 18) sts rem for each shoulder.

Place right shoulder sts on stitch holder or waste yarn.

Left Shoulder and Front

Next row: Purl.

Next RS row (dec): Sl 1, k2, ssk, knit to end—1 st decreased.

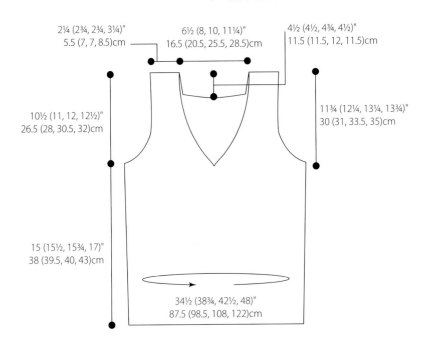

2¼ (2¾, 2¾, 3¼)"
5.5 (7, 7, 8.5)cm

6½ (8, 10, 11¼)"
16.5 (20.5, 25.5, 28.5)cm

4½ (4½, 4¾, 4½)"
11.5 (11.5, 12, 11.5)cm

10½ (11, 12, 12½)"
26.5 (28, 30.5, 32)cm

11¾ (12¼, 13¼, 13¾)"
30 (31, 33.5, 35)cm

15 (15½, 15¾, 17)"
38 (39.5, 40, 43)cm

34½ (38¾, 42½, 48)"
87.5 (98.5, 108, 122)cm

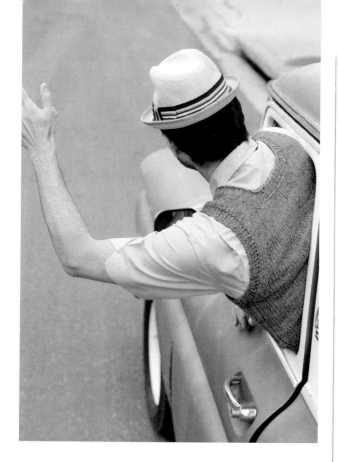

Continue in St st and rep dec row every 4th row (every other RS row) 3 (1, 3, 3) more time(s)—10 (12, 12, 14) sts rem.

Work 35 (37, 39, 41) rows even in St st, ending with a WS row.

Next RS row (inc): Sl 1, k1, kfb, knit to end—1 st increased.

Continue in St st and rep inc row every 4th row (every other RS row) 6 (7, 8, 9) more times—17 (20, 21, 24) sts.

Work 3 rows even in St st.

Next row (inc 2 sts): Sl 1, k1, kfb, knit to last 4 sts, kfb, k3.

Work 1 row even.

Next row (inc 1 st): Sl 1, k1, kfb, knit to end.

Work 1 row even.

Rep last 4 rows 3 (4, 4, 6) more times, then rep the first inc row (2 sts increased) 1 (0, 1, 0) more time(s)—31 (35, 38, 45) sts.

Break yarn and place stitches on waste yarn or stitch holder.

Right Shoulder and Front

Place right shoulder stitches on larger needles.

Examine all of your remaining balls of yarn to see if you have one that starts at the same point of the progression as your right shoulder (going from the same direction as your original ball—inside or outside of the center-pull ball). If not, you can simply unwind one of the balls until you hit the appropriate point—don't worry; you can use up that bit later with the edging or between balls on the body.

With WS facing, join yarn. Purl 1 row.

Next RS row (dec): Sl 1, knit to last 5 sts, k2tog, k3—1 st decreased.

Continue in St st and rep dec row every 4th row (every other RS row) 3 (1, 3, 3) more time(s)—10 (12, 12, 14) sts rem.

Work 35 (37, 39, 41) rows even in St st, ending with a WS row.

Next RS row (inc): Sl 1, k1, knit to last 4 sts, kfb, k3—1 st increased.

Continue in St st and rep inc row every 4th row (every other RS row) 6 (7, 8, 9) more times—17 (20, 21, 24) sts.

Work 3 rows even in St st.

Next row (inc 2 st): Sl 1, k1, kfb, knit to last 4 sts, kfb, k3.

Work 1 row even.

Next row (inc 1 st): Sl 1, knit to last 4 sts, kfb, k3.

Rep last 4 rows 3 (4, 4, 6) more times, then rep first inc row (2 sts increased) 1 (0, 1, 0) more time(s)—31 (35, 38, 45) sts.

Join Front and Back

Remove waste yarn CO edge and place live sts on smaller needles as you go.

NOTES: From this point on, only slip the first stitch and knit the last stitch where explicitly noted.

If the color of the back and your current yarn are quite different, on the next round, you can join another ball that's closer to the original color and alternate between the two for a few rows.

Starting with the WS of the right shoulder, sl 1, purl to end of right shoulder, pm, CO 12, pm (side sts), being careful not to twist CO, join to back and purl across back sts, pm, CO 12, pm (side sts). Place left shoulder sts on smaller needle, being careful not to twist, join to back and purl to last st, k1—145 (163,179, 203) sts.

Finish Shaping the V

NOTE: At this point, the vest is gonna look a little freaky—more like a weird sports bra than a men's vest. Don't fret!

Rows 1, 3, 5 & 7 (RS): Sl 1, k1, kfb, knit to side marker, p1, k1, p3, k2, p3, k1, p1, knit to next side marker, p1, k1, p3, k2, p3, k1, p1, knit to last 4 sts, kfb, k3—153 (171, 187, 211) sts. Do not turn at end of last row.

Rows 2, 4 & 6 (WS): Sl 1, knit the knit sts and purl the purl sts to the last st, k1.

Join in the Round

Without turning work, pm for beg of rnd, join front sections and continue as below across other front section, working the remainder in the round.

Body

K1, p1, knit to side marker, continue in established pattern to last 2 sts, p1, k1.

Continue even in established pattern until piece measures 18 (19, 20, 22)" (45.5 [48.5, 51, 56]cm) from back neck bind-off, or 3" (7.5cm) shorter than desired length.

Change to smaller 24" (60cm) needles and work 3" (7.5cm) in k2, p2 ribbing and dec (inc, inc, inc) 1 st on first rnd—152 (172, 188, 212) sts.

BO in pattern.

Arm Edging

With smaller 16" (40cm) needles and RS facing, pick up and knit 1 st in each CO st at bottom of armpit, then 1 st in each slipped st around the edge (or 1 st for every

2 rows, if you neglected the slipped-stitch edging). Join for working in the rnd, pm for beg of rnd.

Work 5 rnds in k1, p1 ribbing (if you have a odd number of sts, knit tog your last and first sts to get an even number on the first rnd). BO in pattern. Starting with a similar place in the color progression of the yarn, repeat on other armhole.

Neckband

With RS facing, starting at right-hand corner of back neck, pick up and knit 1 st in each bound-off st of back neck edge only through the top edge of the little chain formed by the BO (you'll leave the bottom half of each chain visible on the RS to make an edging that matches the vertical pick up edge), at the end of the back neck BO edge, pm, pick up and knit 1 st in each slipped st (or every other row if you neglected the slipped-stitch edging) through both legs of the edging to center of V, pm, pick up and knit the same number of sts along left front and back neck edge same as right, pm for beg of rnd. Join for working in rnds.

Work 1 rnd in k1, p1 ribbing (if you have a odd number of st, knit tog the last st and first sts to get an even number).

Next Rnd (dec): *Ssk, work in established pattern to 2 sts before marker, k2tog; rep from * twice more—6 sts decreased; 2 at each corner of the back neck and 2 sts at the bottom of the V.

Work 1 rnd even.

Next Rnd (dec): Work in pattern to 2 sts before V-neck marker, ssk, k2tog, work in pattern to end—2 sts decreased.

Rep last rnd once more.

BO in pattern.

John Thornton Scarf

John Thornton Scarf

The Call of the Wild

With its canine hero and a cast of human masters that run from responsibly attentive to dangerously ignorant to downright malignant, the appearance of the good-hearted John Thornton (and his equally kind and loving canine companions) late in *The Call of the Wild* is a welcome relief. And the love story between John Thornton and Buck is something no dog person can resist.

With the warmth and bulk to battle a Yukon winter and a weight perfect for traveling light, this quick-knitting masculine cabled scarf is at once rustic and sophisticated. The yarn's novel construction yields a fabric both warm and weightless, and its shaggy profile gives the scarf an instant weathered appearance just right for an outdoorsman. The irregular cabled border and intricate knot cables make it fun to knit without crossing into vexatious. If you prefer a crisper cable, substitute a smooth bulky plied yarn instead.

SIZE
9" (23cm) × 72" (183cm)

MATERIALS
3 skeins Blue Sky Alpacas *Techno* (68% baby alpaca, 10% extra-fine merino, 22% silk; 120 yd./109m per 1.75oz./50g). Shown in 1973 Rogue.

Alpaca fiber blown into fine silk mesh tube.

US 10 (6mm) needles, *or size needed to obtain gauge*

Cable needle or spare dpn

GAUGE
14 sts × 16 rows = 4" (10cm) in St st

Instructions

CO 38 sts.

Row 1: Sl 1 wyif, [k4, p4] 4 times, k5.

Row 2: Sl 1 wyif, [p4, k4] 4 times, p4, k1.

Rows 3–6: Rep Rows 1 and 2 two more times.

Rows 7–22: Work Chart 1 once.

Rows 23–106: Work Chart 2 three times.

Rows 107–122: Work Chart 1 once.

Rows 123–178: Work Chart 2 twice.

Rows 179–194: Work Chart 1 once.

Rows 195–278: Work Chart 2 three times.

Rows 279–295: Work Chart 1 Rows 5–16 once, then Rows 1–5 once.

Rows 296–300: Rep Row 2, then Rows 1 and 2 two more times.

BO in patt.

Finishing

Weave in ends and block to finished dimensions or to achieve desired appearance.

Chart 1

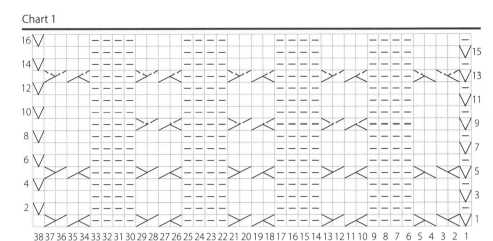

Chart 2

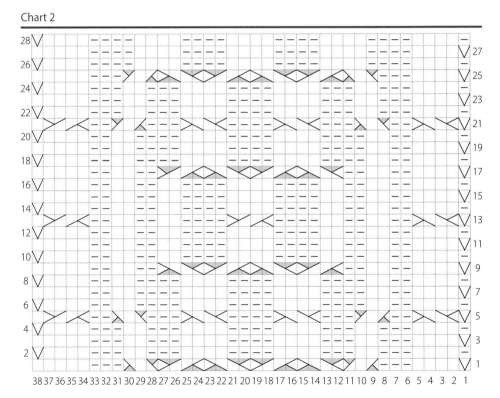

Key to Charts 1 and 2

2/1 LPC
2/1lpc
(RS) Sl 2 to cn, hold to front, p1, k2 from cn

2/1 RPC
2/1rpc
(RS) Sl 1 to cn, hold to back, k2, p1 from cn

2/2 LPC
2/2lpc
(RS) Sl 2 to cn, hold to front, p2, k2 from cn

2/2 RPC
2/2rpc
(RS) Sl 2 to cn, hold to back, k2, p2 from cn

2/2 RC
2/2rc
(RS) Sl 2 to cn, hold to back, k2, k2 from cn

2/2 LC
2/2lc
(RS) Sl 2 to cn, hold to front, k2, k2 from cn

Knit
k on RS, p on WS

Purl
p on RS, k on WS

Slip
sl 1 wyif

Sydney Carton Cowl

Sydney Carton Cowl

A Tale of Two Cities

The most unnerving scenes in *A Tale of Two Cities* include the cold-blooded, determined Madame Defarge, who "knitted on with the steadfastness of Fate." The vengeful Defarge, with her ever-growing knitted register of enemies of the Republic, may have been Dickens' invention, but she was rooted in the historic *Tricoteuses*, the market women who were powerful in the early days of the French Revolution, but were later consigned to form an audience at the daily executions, where they must have looked particularly *sang-froid*, impassively working at their needles before the endless parade at the guillotine, "where they were to sit knitting, knitting, counting dropping heads."

Knit with a Defarge-inspired secret code, this cowl (for protecting one's neck, *naturellement*) celebrates *A Tale of Two Cities* with evocative quotes for both Madame Defarge and her opposite, Sydney Carton, Charles Darnay's doppelganger and savior.

The alphabet is Morse code, with bobbles for dots and star stitches for dashes.

Knit the version here, or take inspiration from Thérèse Defarge herself and use the coded alphabet to make your own secret registry of enemies. But take a warning from her violent end and limit your vengeance to your knitting!

SIZE
Adult

MATERIALS
1 skein Malabrigo *Merino Worsted* (100% merino wool, 205 yd./190m per 3.5oz./100g skein). Shown in 125 Mariposa.

Very soft, airy worsted Merino single with interesting kettle-dyed color variation.

US 7 (4.5mm) circular needles, 16" (40cm) length, *or size needed to obtain gauge*

GAUGE
19 sts × 25 rows = 4" (10cm) in St st

Instructions

NOTES: To use one instead of both quotes, work 10 rnds of St st instead of 2 before and after the chart, and work 5 rnds of St st instead of 3 between each line.

This cowl is worked from the top down. Use the cast-on edge as the top edge for the Morse Code message to read properly.

CO 90 sts. Join for working in the rnd, pm for beg of rnd.

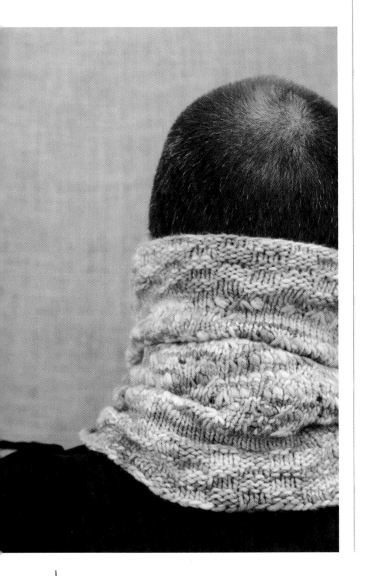

Edging

Rnds 1 & 2: *K3, p3; rep from * around.

Rnds 3–5: *P3, k3; rep from * around.

Rnds 6–10: Rep Rnds 1–5.

Rnds 11 & 12: Rep Rnds 1 and 2.

Rnds 13 & 14: Knit.

Rnds 15–36: Work Madame Defarge chart, knitting to the end of the rnd when reaching the end of chart rows.

NOTE: The Morse code in the Madame Defarge chart spells out:

MADAME DEFARGE
KNITTED WITH
NIMBLE FINGERS
AND STEADY
EYEBROWS AND
SAW NOTHING

Rnds 37 & 38: Knit.

Rnds 39–67: Work Sydney Carton chart, kntting to the end of the rnd when reaching the end of chart rows.

NOTE: The Morse code in the Sydney Carton chart spells out:

IT IS A FAR FAR
BETTER THING THAT
I DO THAN I HAVE
EVER DONE . . . IT IS A
FAR FAR BETTER
REST THAT I GO TO
THAN I HAVE EVER
KNOWN

Rnds 68 & 69: Knit.

Rnds 70–81: Rep Rnds 1–12.

BO in pattern.

Custom Message Tips

To keep everything straight with minimal fuss:

- Start each line with a [k2tog, yo].
- Separate letters with 2 knit sts.
- Separate words with a [k2tog, yo].
- Use three [k2tog, yo] in a row to designate a pause or the end of a phrase.
- Knit 3 rnds between each line.

If you want to encode a different message in your cowl, use the Morse code chart to develop your own pattern.

Morse Code Chart

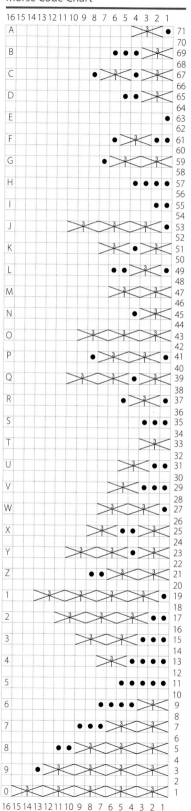

Madame Defarge Chart

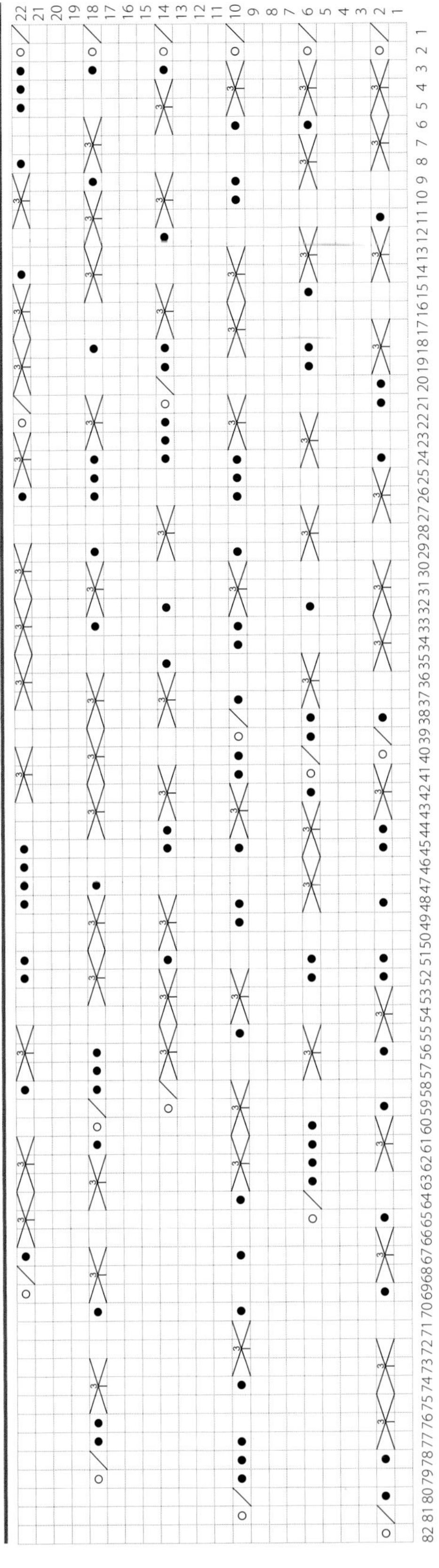

Sydney Carton Chart

Key

●	**Knot**	(kfb) twice in same st-4sts pass 2nd, 3rd and 4th sts over first st and off needle-1st rem.
☐		Knit
╱		k2tog
⧓	**Star Stitch**	k3tog leaving sts on needle, yo, k3tog again through same 3 sts
○		yo

Dorian Gray Fingerless Gloves

The Picture of Dorian Gray

Admiring the rather masculine patterns of the Tess Fingerless Gloves, I knew I had to make a man's version—and what better subject than the dashing, diabolical dandy, Dorian Gray? These gloves use the same charts from the Tess Fingerless Gloves, but at a heavier gauge and minus the frilly cuff. The result is both elegant and masculine. Choose a colorwork cuff and edging, or show off your hand-dyed sock yarn in a simpler version with plain ribbed details.

SIZE
Men's S/M (L/XL)

MATERIALS
Colorwork version:

MC: 1 skein Louet Gems *Sport* (100% superwash Merino, 225 yd./205m per 3.5oz./100g). Shown in 53 Caribou.

CC: 1 skein Louet Gems *Sport*. Shown in 43 Pewter.

Soft, machine washable high-twist 3-ply with soft luster and excellent definition.

1-color version: 1 skein Interlacements *Tiny Toes* (100% superwash Merino, 185 yd./169m per 1.75oz./50g)

Hand-dyed, machine washable high-twist 2-ply with excellent definition.

US 2 (2.75mm) dpns, 2 short circulars, or 1 long circular for Magic Loop

Colorwork version only: US 3 (3.25mm) dpns, 2 short circulars, or 1 long circular for Magic Loop, *or size needed to obtain gauge*

Scrap yarn or large safety pin to hold thumb stitches

Stitch markers

GAUGE
26 sts × 40 rnds = 4" (10cm) in St st on larger needles

Instructions

Wrist

With smaller needles and MC, CO 48 (60) sts. Join for working in the rnd, pm for beg of rnd.

1-color Version

Work 3" (7.5cm) in k2, p2 ribbing.

Knit 5 rnds.

Colorwork Version

Work 3" (7.5cm) in k2, p2 ribbing.

Change to larger needles. Work Colorwork Chart, changing back to smaller needles on last rnd.

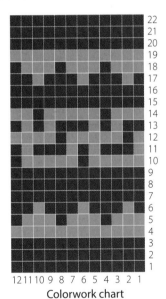

Colorwork chart

Hand

The hand is the same for both versions. Divide the stitches evenly into front and back. With 2 short circulars or Magic Loop, the division will take care of itself. With dpns, place 24 (30) sts on one needle, and divide the remaining sts between two other needles.

NOTE: The first rnd of the chart adds a stitch.

All the action (both the lace and thumb gusset increases) occurs on the odd rounds, whereas all of the even rounds are knit plain.

Right Hand

Rnd 1: Work Diamond Lace chart over first 24 (30) sts, knit to end—49 (61) sts.

Rnd 2 & all even-numbered rnds: Knit.

Rnds 3–13 (odd-numbered rnds only): Work Diamond Lace Chart over first 25 (31) sts, knit to end.

Rnd 15: Work Diamond Lace Chart over first 25 (31) sts, k2, yo, k2, pm, knit to end—50 (62) sts.

Rnds 17–31 (35) (odd-numbered rnds only): Work Diamond Lace Chart over first 25 (31) sts, k2, yo, knit to 2 sts before marker, yo, knit to end—66 (82) sts.

Rnd 33 (37): Work Diamond Lace Chart over first 25 (31) sts, place next 21 (25) sts on scrap yarn for thumb, knit to end—45 (57) sts.

Rnds 35 (39)–45 (odd-numbered rnds only): Work Diamond Lace Chart over first 25 (31) sts, knit to end.

Left Hand

Rnds 1: Work Diamond Lace chart over first 24 (30) sts, knit to end—49 (61) sts.

Rnd 2 & all even-numbered rnds: Knit.

Diamond Lace Chart

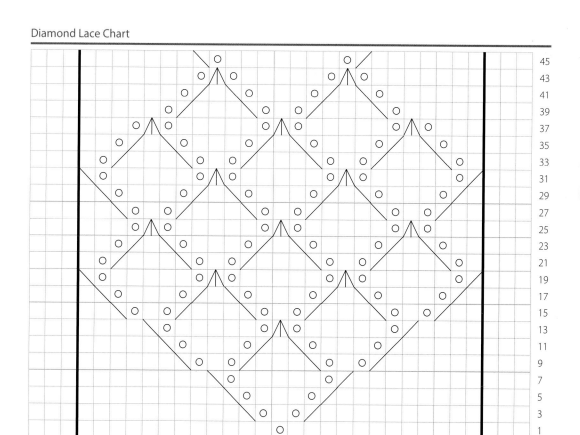

Note: Chart shows odd-numbered (patterned) rows only; knit all even-numbered rows.

End L/XL   End S/M

Beg S/M   Beg L/XL

Key to Diamond Lace Chart

⋀	sk2p
☐	k
╱	k2tog
╲	ssk
○	yo

Rnds 3–13 (odd-numbered rnds only): Work Diamond Lace chart over first 25 (31) sts, knit to end.

Rnd 15: Work Diamond Lace chart over first 25 (31) sts, knit to last 4 sts, pm, k2 yo, k2—50 (62) sts.

Rnds 17–31 (35) (odd-numbered rnds only): Work Diamond Lace chart over first 25 (31) sts, knit to marker, k2, yo, knit to last 2 sts, yo, k2—66 (82) sts.

Rnd 33 (37): Work Diamond Lace Chart over first 25 (31) sts, k20 (26), place next 21 (25) sts on scrap yarn for thumb 45 (57) sts.

Rnd 35 (39)–45 (odd-numbered rnds only): Work Diamond Lace chart over first 25 (31) sts, knit to end.

Top Edge (Both Hands)

Rnds 46 & 47: Knit.

Rnd 48: Knit to last 2 sts, k2tog—44 (56) sts.

1-color Version

Rnds 49 & 50: Knit.

Work 6 rnds in k2, p2 ribbing.

BO in rib.

Colorwork Version

Change to larger needles.

Rnds 49–51: Work Rnds 17–19 of Colorwork Chart.

Change to smaller needles.

Rnd 52: With MC, knit.

Rnd 53: With MC, purl.

Rnd 54: With CC, knit.

Rnd 55: With CC, purl.

Rnd 56: With MC, BO knitwise.

Thumb

Place thumb sts on smaller dpns.

With MC, pick up and knit 2 sts over crotch of thumb, knit to 1 st before crotch, k2tog—22 (26) sts. Join for working in the rnd, pm for beg of rnd.

Next rnd: Ssk, knit to end—21 (25) sts.

Knit 4 rnds even.

1-color Version

Next rnd: [K2, p2] 4 (5) times, k2, p1, p2tog—20 (24) sts.

Work 2 more rnds in k2, p2 ribbing. BO in patt.

Colorwork Version

Next rnd: With CC, knit.

Next rnd: With CC, purl.

Next rnd: With MC, BO knitwise.

Finishing

Weave in ends. Soak in hot water, spin/press to remove excess water. Lay flat to dry.

Billy Pilgrim Socks

Billy Pilgrim Socks

Slaughterhouse-Five

S piral Socks—refined versions of the tube sock—appeared in several WWII "Knit Your Bit" pamphlets. Easy yet entertaining to knit, these heelless socks can be rotated around the foot as needed to minimize and/or accommodate heel wear, making them ideal for servicemen. Avoiding a heel also shaves knitting time and makes the size very flexible, critical when you're knitting for a stranger. But the real charm of the spiral sock is that it can be easily adapted for any gauge yarn, and knit to any length without regard to heel placement, allowing you to make the most of whatever yarn you have on hand.

The limitless yarn and design potential of spiral socks makes them perfect for "unstuck in time" *Slaughterhouse-Five* protagonist Billy Pilgrim. Knit them in plain wool for his WWII POW appearances, jaunty stripes for his postwar jumps, or silky superwash Merino for his escapades on Tralfamadore (though, technically, I suppose he was barefoot there . . .).

Instructions are included for three general weights: aran/chunky, light worsted/dk, and midweight sock yarn. You can adapt to any other yarn simply by casting on more or fewer stitches, always working in increments of 4 (or as appropriate to your custom pattern). I used a 4-stitch, 4-row repeat because it's a snap to remember, but the pattern can easily be wider or travel faster— just shift the pattern a stitch at a time at regular intervals and you're set.

The pattern includes a pair of opposite spirals. Use one pattern for each sock for a mirrored pair or the same pattern for both socks if you want to make identical twins (easier if you're knitting them two-at-a-time). I've also included a fun zigzag variation.

SIZE

Adult S (M, L)

Roughly 16 (18, 20)" /(40.5 [45.5, 51]cm) long for crew length

S = up to a Men's US 7/Women's US 9/Euro 42

M = up to Men's US 10/Women's US 12/Euro 44

L = Men's US 10/Women's US 11–13/Euro 46–48

MATERIALS

Yarn

Aran/Chunky: 200 (250, 300)yd./(183 [229, 274]m) Vera Videnovich *Handspun Sport-to-Chunky 2-ply* (100% wool, approx. 50yd./45m per 1oz./28g). Shown in Eucalyptus leaf-dyed.

Sturdy thick-and-thin 2-ply is kettle dyed before handspinning for soft color variation.

DK/Light Worsted: 2 balls JoJoLand *Rhythm* (100% wool, 110yd./100m per 1.75oz./50g). Shown in M24.

Classic worsted self-striping 3-ply, each ply a different color for complex, tweedy-looking color progressions. Also in a superwash line.

Sock: 1 skein Blue Moon Fiber Arts *Socks that Rock mediumweight* (100% Superwash Merino, 380yd./347m per 5.5oz./155g). Shown in Gertrude Skein.

Hand-dyed, soft machine washable high-twist 3-ply with soft luster and excellent definition.

Aran/Chunky: US 4 (3.5mm) dpns, 2 short circulars, or long circular for Magic Loop, *or size needed to obtain gauge*

DK/Light Worsted: US 3 (3.25mm) dpns, 2 short circulars, or long circular for Magic Loop, *or size needed to obtain gauge*

Sock: US 1 (2.25mm) dpns, 2 short circulars, or long circular for Magic Loop, *or size needed to obtain gauge*

GAUGE

Aran/Chunky: 17 sts × 24 rows = 4" (10cm) in St st

DK/Light Worsted: 25 sts × 32 rows = 4" (10cm) in St st

Sock: 31sts × 42 rows = 4" (10cm) in St st

Pattern Notes

Mirrored Spiral Patterns (multiple of 4 sts)

Ribbed Spiral #1

Rnds 1–4: *K3, p1; rep from * around.

Rnds 5–8: *P1, k3; rep from * around.

Rnds 9–12: K1, *p1, k3; rep from * to last 3 sts, p1, k2.

Rnds 13–16: K2, *p1, k3; rep from * to last 2 sts, p1, k1.

Rep Rnds 1–16 for patt.

Ribbed Spiral #2

Rnds 1–4: *K3, p1; rep from * around.

Rnds 5–8: K2, *p1, k3; rep from * to last 2 sts, p1, k1.

Rnds 9–12: K1, *p1, k3; rep from * to last 3 sts, p1, k2.

Rnds 13–16: *P1, k3; rep from * around.

Rep Rnds 1–16 for patt.

Zigzag Variation

Alternate between both sets of your chosen pattern (start with opposite set on each sock for mirrored design).

Instructions

Leg

Aran/Chunky: CO 40 (48, 56) sts.

DK/Light Worsted: CO 48 (56, 64) sts.

Sock: CO 56 (64, 72) sts.

Join for working in the rnd, pm for beg of rnd. Beg desired pattern and work until piece measures 14 (16, 18)" (35.5 [40.5, 45.5]cm) long, or 2" (5cm) less than desired length.

Eyelet Spiral Variation

Try this eyelet spiral variation for dress socks. The built-in ventilation makes a nice warmer-weather sock as well.

Eyelet Spiral #1 (multiple of 4 sts)

Rnds 1–4: *K2, k2tog, yo; rep from * around.

Rnds 5–8: *Yo, k2, k2tog; rep from * around.

Rnds 9–12: *K2tog, yo, k2; rep from * around.

Rnds 13–16: K1, *k2tog, yo, k2; rep from * to last 3 sts, k2tog, yo, k1.

Rep Rnds 1–16 for patt.

Eyelet Spiral #2

Rnds 1–4: *K2, k2tog, yo; rep from * around.

Rnds 5–8: K1, *k2tog, yo, k2; rep from * to last 3 sts, k2tog, yo, k1.

Rnds 9–12: *K2tog, yo, k2; rep from * around.

Rnds 13–16: *Yo, k2, k2tog; rep from * around.

Rep Rnds 1–16 for patt.

Toe

Work 1 (3, 4) rnd(s) in St st.

Next rnd: (K6, k2tog) across rnd—35 (42, 49) sts for Aran/Chunky; 42 (49, 56) sts for DK/Light Worsted; and 49 (56, 63) sts for Sock.

Work 2 (3, 3) rnd(s) even.

Next rnd: (K5, k2tog) across rnd—30 (36, 42) sts for Aran/Chunky; 36 (42, 48) sts for DK/Light Worsted; and 42 (48, 54) sts for Sock.

Work 2 (3, 3) rnd(s)s even.

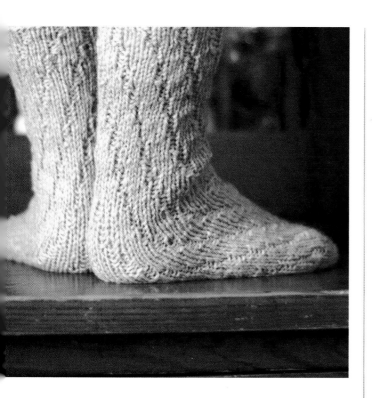

Next rnd: (K4, k2tog) across rnd—25 (30, 35) sts for Aran/Chunky; 30 (35, 40) sts for DK/Light Worsted; and 35 (40, 45) sts for Sock.

Work 2 (3, 3) rnd(s) even.

Next rnd: (K3, k2tog) across rnd—20 (24, 28) sts for Aran/Chunky; 24 (28, 32) sts for DK/Light Worsted; and 28 (32, 36) sts for Sock.

Work 2 (3, 3) rnd(s) even.

Next rnd: (K2, k2tog) across rnd—15 (18, 21) sts for Aran/Chunky; 18 (21, 24) sts for DK/Light Worsted; and 21 (24, 27) sts for Sock.

Work 2 (3, 3) rnd(s) even.

Next rnd: [K1, k2tog] across rnd—10 (12, 14) sts for Aran/Chunky; 12 (14, 16) sts for DK/Light Worsted; and 14 (16, 18) sts for Sock.

Break yarn and thread tail through rem sts. Pull tight to secure and fasten off on WS. Weave in ends.

4

In Which We Knit

for Children

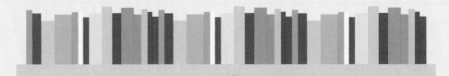

Laura Pinafore

Little House on the Prairie

When I was a little girl, I was bananas for Laura Ingalls. I love the adventure, the pioneer spirit, the celebration of frugality, DIY, and craft. Of course, I wouldn't have phrased it in that way, but I loved both making things by hand and pinching pennies at a very early age, so a whole series of books that elevated scrimping, denounced frivolity, had a heroine who had to struggle to be good, *and* involved all kinds of old-timey stuff—well, that was my idea of a good time.

Rereading these children's classics as an adult, I'm still thrilled at the thrifty ingenuity and can-do spirit of the age. This waste-not, want-not dress is a celebration of that pioneer philosophy, perfect for all those leftover odds and ends that seem to multiply in everyone's stash. And because it's meant to be worn over a shirt, you're free to include hard-wearing scratchy scraps.

SIZE
Child 1/2 (3/4, 5/6, 7/8, 9/10, 11/12)

MATERIALS
About 500 (600, 700, 800, 1000, 1200) yd./457 (549, 640, 731, 914, 1097)m random worsted weight odds and ends.

Red sample used dozens of random odds and ends. Green sample (size 5/6) used 1 skein each of Cascade 220 in Turtle and Granny Smith, 2 balls of Valley Yarns Cold Spring in Forest Canopy, 1 skein of Lion Brand Baby Wool in Pear.

US 8 (5mm) circular needles, 24" (60cm) length for smaller range of sizes, 32" (80cm) length for larger range of sizes, *or size needed to obtain gauge*

US 7 (4.5mm) needles

2 buttons, ½" (13mm)

Sewing needle and thread

Tapestry needle

GAUGE
16 sts × 22 rows = 4" (10cm) in St st on larger needles

Pattern Notes

If 1 or both of your strands are multicolored, your stripes will be softer and require less planning, even if the total range of colors is quite broad. Similarly, selecting several yarns in the same color range will produce a subdued, harmonious look. Solid color strands in contrasting colors will produce bolder stripes. For a graphic, modern look, you might alternate between just two solid colors throughout. For a rich painterly effect, choose colors that are quite similar, and include yarns or blends that produce a halo, such as angora, alpaca, kid mohair, and so on. Or carry 1 strand of the same yarn throughout, alternating with dozens of different little odds and ends.

Instructions

Always alternate between 2 colors. In the garter yoke and hem, you'll alternate every 2 rows/rnds; in the stockinette body, alternate every rnd. You can switch out either color at any time.

Yoke

With smaller needles, CO 70 (75, 80, 85, 85, 95) sts.

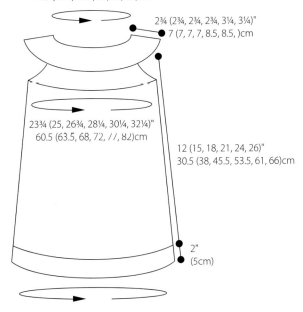

16¼ (17½, 18¾, 20, 20, 22½)"
41.5 (44.5, 47.5, 51, 51, 57)cm

2¾ (2¾, 2¾, 2¾, 3¼, 3¼)"
7 (7, 7, 7, 8.5, 8.5,)cm

23¾ (25, 26¾, 28¼, 30¼, 32¼)"
60.5 (63.5, 68, 72, 77, 82)cm

12 (15, 18, 21, 24, 26)"
30.5 (38, 45.5, 53.5, 61, 66)cm

2"
(5cm)

29¾ (32, 35¾, 39¼, 42¼, 45¼)"
75.5 (81.5, 91, 99.5, 107.5, 115)cm

Row 1: Sl 1, knit to end.

Rep last row 20 (20, 20, 20, 24, 24) more times and change colors every 2 rows.

At the same time, inc 15 sts evenly across every 5th row 4 (4, 4, 4, 5, 5) times—130 (135, 140, 145, 160, 170) sts.

Divide for Armholes

Change to larger needles.

Slipping first st, BO 5 sts, k 19 (20, 21, 22, 24, 26), BO 25 (25, 26, 27, 31, 32), k 37 (40, 41, 42, 45, 49), BO 25 (25, 26, 27, 31, 32), knit to end—75 (80, 83, 89, 93, 101) sts. Join for working in the rnd, pm for beg of rnd.

Change colors. K 19 (20, 21, 22, 24, 26), CO 5 (5, 6, 6, 7, 7), pm, CO 5 (5, 6, 6, 7, 7), k 37 (40, 41, 42, 45, 49), CO 5 (5, 6, 6, 7, 7), pm, CO 5 (5, 6, 6, 7, 7), knit to end—95 (100, 107, 113, 121, 129) sts.

Change colors. Sl 1, k18 (19, 20, 21, 23, 25), p10 (10, 12, 12, 14, 14), k37 (40, 41, 42, 45, 49), p10 (10, 12, 12, 14, 14), knit to end.

Body

From this point, knit all rnds and alternate between colors every round. If you like, work joggless stripes (see sidebar).

Cont St st and **at the same time** kfb in the stitch immediately before and after each side marker every 10th rnd 6 (7, 9, 11, 12, 13) times—119 (128, 143, 157, 169, 181) sts.

Work even until St st portion is 12 (15, 18, 21, 24, 26)" (30.5 [38, 45.5, 53.5, 61, 66] cm).

Hem

Change colors. No need to worry about row jog after this point. Beginning with a purl round and alternating colors every 2 rnds, work a total of 14 rnds in garter (purl 1 rnd, knit 1 rnd), then BO pwise.

Jogless Stripes

To prevent the row jog at the end of the round, work the first 2 stitches of each color change loosely then knit until you work back around to that first stitch. Slip that first stitch of your current color before switching to the next color. This method creates the impression of a continuous stripe, but it also shifts the start of your round 1 stitch to the left every round, and it does have a tendency to make a diagonal line across your work if you're not really careful with your tension (that's why you work the first stitches nice and loose to give you some room to futz with the stitches at the jog line and tidy them up).

Pocket

With smaller needles, CO 16 (18, 20, 22, 24, 26) sts.

Sl 1, knit to end.

Rep last row, changing colors every 2 rows, until the pocket is roughly square.

BO, leaving a tail for sewing on the pocket. Weave in starting end.

Sew pocket on center front either 1–2" (2.5–5cm) below yoke or just below waist. You could also make 2 pockets and place them at hip level on each side of front.

Finishing

Overlap tabbed side of yoke and sew buttons through both layers (buttons are decorative; neck is wide enough to easily fit overhead).

Alternatively, sew buttons to the flat side and simply push them through the garter tab—buttonholes aren't really necessary with wee buttons.

Oskar Pullover

The Tin Drum

In 1980, a year after my family moved to suburban Houston, the cable industry was in its infancy and all of the handful of movies on offer each month were in heavy rotation. As a latchkey kid with few friends (and MTV still a year away) I had ample opportunity to overdose on cable movies, especially in the summertime.

Thus at age 10 or 11, *The Blue Lagoon, Somewhere in Time, Breaking Glass*, and *Alien* all got an unwholesome portion of my attention. But the movie that made the most haunting impression on me was also my first foreign film, *The Tin Drum*. Its impact was made all the more powerful from my lack of access—once it left cable, it completely vanished for me. There was no Internet, so my film world only reached as far as the little video rental rack at our neighborhood grocery store.

Almost a decade later, I stumbled across a paperback copy of *The Tin Drum* in a used book store, and I brought it home. I'd always been an enthusiastic, responsive reader, but that book just annihilated me. It's still one of my favorites.

The diminutive Oskar Matzerath, the book's sometime protagonist and Peter Pan's dark doppelganger, is the inspiration for this simple boyish sweater. The slow, subtle color progressions in the yarn give the garment a faded, nostalgic look, and the wee triangle pattern inset is a little wink to Oskar's ubiquitous toy drums. The yarn is lightweight, and the sweater is the same in the front and back, making it a good choice for little ones.

SIZE
Child 1/2 (3/4, 5/6, 7/8, 9/10, 11/12)

MATERIALS
MC: 3 (4, 4, 5, 5, 6) balls Valley Yarns *Cold Spring* (39% wool/36% fine acrylic/25% baby alpaca; 108 yd./99m per 1.75oz./50g ball). Shown in 02 Fall Harvest.

CC: 1 (1, 1, 1, 2, 2) ball(s) Valley Yarns *Cold Spring*. Shown in 06 Forest Canopy.

Lofty, fuzzy wool-blend aran with very long, very subtle color progressions.

US 6 (4mm) circular needles, 16" (40cm) length for larger sizes; dpns or long circular Magic Loop for smaller sizes

US 7 (4.5mm) circular needles, 16" (40cm) length for larger sizes; dpns or long circular for Magic Loop for smaller sizes

US 7 (4.5mm) circular needles, 24" (60cm) length, *or size needed to obtain gauge*

Tapestry needle

Stitch markers

GAUGE

18 sts × 27 rnds = 4" (10cm) in St st on larger needles

Instructions

Before you get started, set aside the two most similar balls for the sleeves. On the smaller sizes, you can work the sleeves before you complete the torso and then use the remainder to finish the torso.

Collar

With smaller needles (dpns or Magic Loop) and MC, CO 68 (72, 76, 80, 84, 88) sts. Join for working in the rnd, pm for beg of rnd.

Work 5 rnds of k1, p1 ribbing.

Raglan Shoulders

Change to larger needles (dpns or Magic Loop).

K10 (11, 12, 12, 13, 13) for sleeve, pm, k24 (25, 26, 28, 29, 31) for back, pm, k10 (11,12,12,13,13) for sleeve, pm, knit rem 24 (25, 26, 28, 29, 31) sts for front.

Working in St st (knit every rnd), change to 24" (60cm) circulars when it's comfortable, and inc on both sides of every marker every other rnd 10 (13, 17, 18, 20, 21) times, working all inc as kfb (8 sts inc'd every other rnd)—148 (176, 212, 224, 244, 256) sts. Work should measure approx 4 (5, 6, 6½, 7, 7½)" (10 [12.5, 15, 16.5, 18, 19]cm) from CO edge, measured along center front.

Divide for Sleeves

Join CC and CO 4 (5, 8, 8, 9, 11) sts for underarm, slip 30 (37, 46, 48, 53, 55) sleeve sts to waste yarn or holder, k44 (51, 60, 64, 69, 73) back sts, CO 4 (5, 8, 8, 9, 11) sts for underarm, slip 30 (37, 46, 48, 53, 55) sleeve sts to

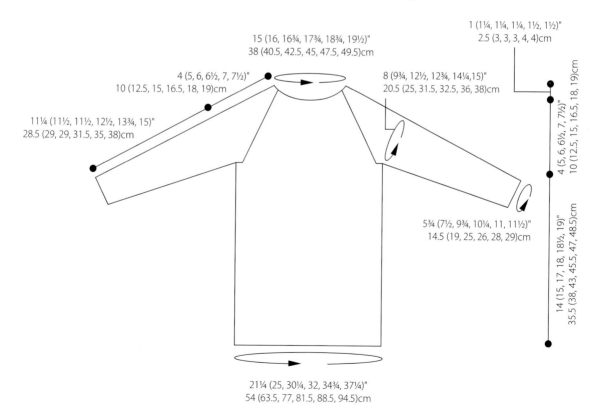

15 (16, 16¾, 17¾, 18¾, 19½)"
38 (40.5, 42.5, 45, 47.5, 49.5)cm

1 (1¼, 1¼, 1¼, 1½, 1½)"
2.5 (3, 3, 3, 4, 4)cm

4 (5, 6, 6½, 7, 7½)"
10 (12.5, 15, 16.5, 18, 19)cm

8 (9¾, 12½, 12¾, 14¼,15)"
20.5 (25, 31.5, 32.5, 36, 38)cm

11¼ (11½, 11½, 12½, 13¾, 15)"
28.5 (29, 29, 31.5, 35, 38)cm

4 (5, 6½, 7, 7½)"
10 (12.5, 15, 16.5, 18, 19)cm

5¾ (7½, 9¾, 10¼, 11, 11½)"
14.5 (19, 25, 26, 28, 29)cm

14 (15, 17, 18, 18½, 19)"
35.5 (38, 43, 45.5, 47, 48.5)cm

21¼ (25, 30¼, 32, 34¾, 37¼)"
54 (63.5, 77, 81.5, 88.5, 94.5)cm

waste yarn or holder, k44 (51, 60, 64, 69, 73) front sts—96 (112, 136, 144, 156, 168) sts.

Body

Work 1 (1, 1½, 1½, 1¾, 2)" (2.5 [2.5, 4, 4, 4.5, 5]cm) of St st in CC.

Join MC and knit 1 rnd.

Next 2 rnds: *K1 in CC, k3 in MC; rep from * to end.

Next 2 rnds: K2 in CC, *k1 in MC, k3 in CC; rep from * to last 2 sts, k1 in MC, k1 in CC.

Knit 1 rnd in CC.

Knit 1 rnd in MC.

Work 1 (1, 1½, 1½, 1¾, 2)" (2.5 [2.5, 4, 4, 4.5, 5]cm) of St st in CC.

Change to MC. Cont in St st until piece measures 12 (13, 15, 16, 16½, 17)" (30.5 [33, 38, 40.5, 42, 43]cm) from CO edge, measured along center front.

Change to smaller needles.

Work 2" (5cm) in k1, p1 ribbing. BO in patt.

Sleeves

Transfer sleeve stitches to larger dpns or long circular for Magic Loop.

Join MC (one of the reserved balls) and pick up and k1 st in the gap between sleeve and body, pick up and k1 st in every st along CO edge, then 1 st in the

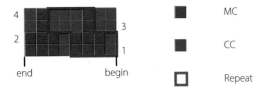

gap between sleeve and opposite side of body, k30 (37, 46, 48, 53, 55) sleeve sts, knit to center of underarm—36 (44, 56, 58, 64, 68) sts.

Join to work in the rnd, pm for beg of rnd.

Working in St st, and dec 1 st at beg and end of every 12th (12th, 10th, 10th, 10th, 10th) rnd 5 (5, 6, 6, 7, 8) times, working k2tog at beg of rnd and ssk at end of rnd—26 (34, 44, 46, 50, 52) sts rem. Work even until sleeve measures 9¼ (9½, 9½, 10½, 11¾, 13)" (23.5 [24, 24, 26.5, 30, 33]cm) from underarm.

Change to smaller needles.

Work 2" (5cm) in k1, p1 ribbing. BO in patt.

Weave in ends. Block to finished measurements.

Edmund Crown/Hat

The Lion, the Witch, and the Wardrobe

For a child, the best part of the magical world of Narnia—with its talking animals, witches, monsters, mythical creatures, secret destinies, and glorious adventures—was that it was just a wardrobe away. I'm sure every child that read *The Chronicles of Narnia* checked strange cupboards as routinely as they checked payphone coin returns—you know, *just in case*. (With the extinction of pay phones, modern kids can at least console themselves with all the extra cupboards of IKEA.)

Inspired by the Pevensie children's secret—and instantly reversible—royalty, this reversible hat features a plain brim that reverses to a golden crown at a moment's notice. Equally suitable for all of the Pevensie children, the hat is named for Edmund, who got sidetracked achieving his destiny, but made good in the end.

SIZE
Child (Youth/Small adult); circumference 18¼ (20¼)" (46.5 [51.5]cm) and length 8¼ (9½)" (21 [24]cm)

MATERIALS
MC: (2) skeins Knit Picks *Swish* (100% superwash Merino wool, 110yd./100m per 1.75oz./50g). Shown in Hollyberry.

CC: 1 (1) skein Knit Picks *Swish*. Shown in Turmeric.

NOTE: Turmeric is no longer available. Cornmeal is an alternative.

Classic plied worsted yarn in soft machine-washable Merino.

US 6 (7) (4 [4.5]mm) 16" (40cm) circulars plus dpns, or long circular for Magic Loop , *or size needed to obtain gauge*

Spare circular needle, the same size or a bit smaller, for seaming the brim

GAUGE
19 (21) sts × 28 (32) rows = 4" (10cm) in St st

Instructions

Brim

Crown side

CO 96 sts with CC. Join for working in the rnd, pm for beg of rnd.

Knit 8 rnds.

Work Chart Rnds 1–11.

Change to MC.

Knit 1 rnd.

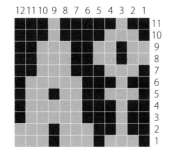

■ MC
□ CC

Plain side

Purl 1 rnd.

Sl 1 wyib, then purl to end (for jogless transition).

P1, sl 1 wyib, then knit to end (for jogless transition).

Knit 19 more rnds.

Weave in ends.

Join Brims

live sts from brim

new sts pu and knit through CO edge

Fold brim along purl rnd with CO edge even with needle. Turn work with crown side facing. With spare circular needle, use working strand to pick up and knit 1 st in each CO st, working into back half of CO edge only—96 sts on each needle.

Turn work with plain side facing and both circular needles held parallel. * (k2tog, using 1 st from each needle) 4 times, (p2tog, using 1 st from each needle) 4 times; rep from * across rnd—96 sts.

Body of Hat

Rnd 1: *K4 p4; rep from * across rnd.

Rep Rnd 1 until ribbing measures 4½ (5½)" (11.5 [14]cm) long.

Crown of Hat

Next rnd: *Ssk, k2tog, p4, k4, p4; rep from * around—84 sts.

Next rnd: *K2, p4, k4, p4; rep from * around.

Next rnd: *K2, p4, ssk, k2tog, p4; rep from * around—72 sts.

Next rnd: *K2, p4; rep from * around.

Next rnd: *K2, p2tog, ssp; rep from * around—60 sts.

Next rnd: *K2, p2; rep from * around.

Next rnd: *K2tog, p2tog; rep from * around—30 sts.

Next rnd: K2tog around—15 sts.

Next rnd: *K2tog; rep from * to last st, k1—8 sts.

Break yarn, thread tail through rem sts. Pull tight to secure and fasten off on WS so hat is reversible.

Finishing

Weave in ends. Block hat to finished measurements. I like to tug vigorously in all directions to even out the colorwork, if necessary (this pattern is fairly simple, so there might not be much need). If it's still lumpy, tug it again while it's damp.

Lyra Hood

Lyra Hood

The Golden Compass

Lyra Belacqua, the pint-sized adventurer of *The Golden Compass,* is a marvelously complex heroine. She is brave, clever, perceptive, loyal, loving—but also willful, impetuous, quick-tempered, and obstinate.

Like the complicated girl it was designed after, this dual-personality hood has different sides. Its rustic exterior conceals a plush alpaca lining—and a secret!

The hood's opening is thrummed with soft hand-dyed Merino combed top; the fabric's stockinette curl rolls the thrummed interior out. Tucked inside the hood's lush red interior—nestled in just the spot to whisper advice and encouragement into one's ear—crouches the hood's secret cargo, a duplicate-stitch Pantalaimon in mouse form.

SIZE
Toddler/Child (Youth/Adult)

MATERIALS
Exterior: 2 skeins Vera Videnovich *Handspun Chunky Single-Ply* (100% wool, 100yd./91m per 2.5oz./71g). Shown in Natural Brown Corriedale.

A lofty rustic thick-and-thin chunky handspun single.

Thrums: 3 oz. Art Club *Hand-dyed Combed Top* (100% unspun Merino wool). Shown in Wolverine.

Soft commercial combed top, kettle dyed in fur colors.

Interior: 1 skein Blue Sky Alpacas *Sport Weight* (100% baby alpaca, 110 yd./100m per 1.75oz./50g). Shown in 511 Red.

Pantalaimon: 1 skein Blue Sky Alpacas *Sport Weight*. Shown in 505 Taupe.

A buttery sportweight alpaca 2-ply with a soft twist.

1 yd./.9 m fine black yarn or embroidery floss for the details.

1 cloak clasp; shown with pewter Drage (Dragon) clasp (see "Resources" in the Epilogue)

US 9 (5.5m) circular needles, 32" (80cm) length, *or size needed to obtain gauge*

US 3 (3.25mm) circular needles, 32" (80cm) length, *or size needed to obtain gauge*

Spare US 3 (3.25mm) or smaller needle

Safety pins, locking stitch markers, or scrap yarn, to mark boundaries for duplicate stitch.

GAUGE

Exterior: 17 sts × 24 rows = 4" (10cm) in St st (without thrums) on larger needles

Interior: 21 sts × 28 rows = 4" (10cm) in St st on smaller needles

Instructions

Thrummed Edging

NOTE: See end of pattern for Thrums tutorial.

CO 60 (90) sts with exterior yarn on larger needles.

Knit 2 rows.

Row 1: Sl 1, T1, *k2, T1; rep from * to last st, k1.

Rows 2 & all even rows: Sl 1, purl to last st, k1.

Row 3: Sl 1, k1, T1, *k2, T1; rep from * to last st, k3.

Row 5: Sl 1, k2, T1, *k2, T1; rep from * to last 2 sts, k2.

Rep Rows 1–6 one (two) more time(s).

Continue in plain St st with a slipped-stitch edge until non-thrummed section is 6 (8)" (15 [20.5]cm), ending with a WS row.

Transfer half the stitches to your spare needle, fold in half so WS are touching, and seam back with 3-needle

bind-off (using the other end of your larger needle to work the BO). Don't weave in the tail yet.

Interior

Using smaller needles and interior yarn, with WS facing and thrummed portion at bottom of work, pick up and knit 75 (111) sts into the row of purl bumps just above your last thrummed row. You'll be picking up 5 sts for every 4 exterior sts.

TIP: If you examine the purl bumps, you see each row is comprised of an upper ridge and an interlacing lower ridge. Pick up and knit 4 sts into the 4 lower bumps in a row, then pick up and knit your 5th st into the upper bump between your last and next lower bumps, thus squeezing in your extra stitch. If your pick up count isn't exact, don't worry—as long as you're within a few stitches, you're fine.

Row 1: Sl 1, purl to last st, k1.

Row 2: Sl 1, knit to end.

Rep last 2 rows for 5½ (7½)" (14 [19]cm) of stockinette with slipped-stitch edging. If you're making the larger size, you use up all your yarn, so just go as far as the yarn takes you, leaving a bit over 1 yd. (.9 m) for the BO. Leave the stitches on the needles while you work Pantalaimon.

Pantalaimon

NOTE: The two charts in this section are oriented sideways because that is how you will work them.

Decide which chart you're using and mark off the stitches you need with safety pins or a running stitch in scrap yarn. Work the chart in duplicate stitch, adding details as you like.

Standing Pantalaimon Chart

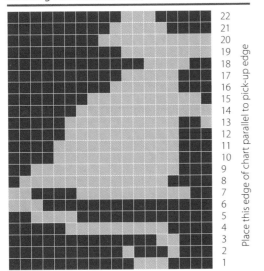

22
21
20
19
18
17
16
15
14
13
12
11
10
9
8
7
6
5
4
3
2
1

Place this edge of chart parallel to pick-up edge

18 17 16 15 14 13 12 11 10 9 8 7 6 5 4 3 2 1

Crouching Pantalaimon Chart

Place this edge of chart parallel to pick-up edge

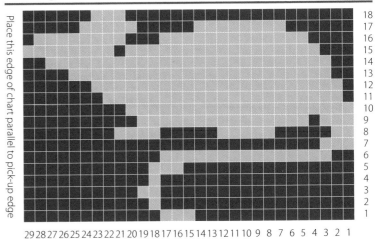

18
17
16
15
14
13
12
11
10
9
8
7
6
5
4
3
2
1

29 28 27 26 25 24 23 22 21 20 19 18 17 16 15 14 13 12 11 10 9 8 7 6 5 4 3 2 1

Interior Back Seam

Transfer half the stitches to a spare needle and, with knit sides facing together, work three-needle bind-off. Use the tail from the exterior back seam to secure interior corner into the exterior.

Edging Bottom

The two layers are slightly different sizes, so pin them together, lining up the back seams, before you begin.

With smaller needles and exterior yarn, with interior facing, pick up and knit 38 (50) sts through both layers.

Row 1: Sl 1, purl to last st, k1.

Row 2: Sl 1, knit to end.

Rep last 2 rows 2 times, then BO.

Finishing

Sew clasp ends 1 (1¾)" (2.5 [4.5]cm) from bottom edge, just between thrums and lining.

Thrums

Thrums are bits of unspun fiber knitted in to produce a fleecy lining on the WS. Hand-dyed commercial Merino combed top (also known as "top" or "tops") makes the best thrums, because carding oil that compresses the fiber gets washed out with the dyeing. If you're using a straight commercial combed top, you might want to give it a soak and dry first for improved loft. Top that's a bit too felted for spinning will do for thrums. Roving will also work, but the looser texture and random fiber arrangement means it doesn't hold together as well.

Tear (don't cut) a 6–8" (15–20.5cm) chunk of top. If the top won't separate readily, tease the fibers apart first, then, with your hands 6–8" (15–20.5cm) apart, pull off a chunk.

Tear each piece lengthwise into 15–20 strips.

Working across the strip, gently attenuate each piece so it's about twice as long. Similar to the pre-drafting that spinners do, this technique adds air, making the thrums loftier and warmer.

Wrap each piece around your index finger and thumb to form a 3" (7.5cm) figure eight of unspun fiber. The rounded ends produce an attractive, smooth fleecy appearance, which is important when your thrums are exposed as they are here. Continue until you have a big pile of them.

T1: Insert needle into stitch kwise, fold thrum around needle and hold ends behind, then wrap your yarn and knit the thrum along with your regular yarn. The appearance is most balanced if you knit English (aka "throw" or carry your working yarn in your right hand). On the next stitch, just leave the thrum where it is and go back to knitting just with your main yarn. You're not carrying the fiber as you would with colorwork, but knitting each thrum in independently. On the next row, as you hit each thrum, work the stitch above it through both the thrum and the yarn to lock it into place.

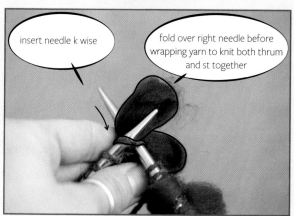

insert needle k wise

fold over right needle before wrapping yarn to knit both thrum and st together

thrum knit with stitch (thrum hides the working yarn)

Scout Cardigan

Scout Cardigan

To Kill a Mockingbird

Scout's clear child's sense of justice makes her an unknowingly wise foil for both the mean big-otry surrounding her father's trial and for the inadvertent injustices imposed upon kids by well-meaning but clueless adults. But mostly, she's just a sweet, tough, fun-loving kid.

This classic two-tone cardigan features a mockingbird motif worked in duplicate stitch (or use intarsia if you're skillful). You can place the birds as shown, omit one, or place them on the breast for a '50s flavor. Or you can change the colors and tweak the chart a bit (for example, add an extra stitch on the top of the head for a bluejay or cardinal) for a favorite sports mascot or state bird.

SIZE
Child 1/2 (3/4, 5/6, 7/8, 9/10, 11/12)

MATERIALS
MC: 2 (3, 3, 4, 4, 4) skeins Louet Gems *Light Worsted* (100% superwash Merino, 175yd./160m per 3.5oz./100g). Shown in 36 Linen Gray.

CC: 1 skein Louet Gems *Light Worsted* (100% superwash Merino, 175yd./160m per 3.5oz./100g). Shown in 22 Black.

Soft machine washable high-twist worsted with subtle luster and excellent definition.

US 6 (4mm) 24" (60cm) circular + dpns, 2 circulars, or long circular for Magic Loop

US 8 (6mm) 24" (60cm) circular + dpns, 2 circulars, or long circular for Magic Loop, *or size needed to obtain gauge*

Stitch markers

Scrap yarn to hold sleeve stitches

7 (7, 8, 9, 10, 11) ¾" (19mm) buttons. Shown in Dritz Bella Buttons BB614 Silver Black Flower buttons.

GAUGE
20 sts × 26 rows = 4" (10cm) in St st on larger needles

Instructions

Neckband

With smaller needles and CC, CO 72 (78, 84, 90, 96, 102) sts.

Rows 1–2: Sl 1, *k1 p1; rep from * to last st, k1.

Row 3 (WS): Sl 1, k1, p1, BO 2 sts in rib, then work in rib to end.

Row 4: Sl 1, work in rib to buttonhole gap, CO 2, then k1, p1, k1.

Row 5: Repeat Row 1.

Place raglan markers on the following row. I like to use a different color marker for the button placket, and work the placket sts as tightly as possible.

Row 6: Sl 1, (k1, p1) twice, k1, pm to divide button placket/front, k8 (9, 10, 11, 12, 13), pm to divide front/sleeve, k11 (12, 13, 14, 15, 16), pm to divide sleeve/back, k22 (24, 26, 28, 30, 32), pm to divide back/sleeve, k11 (12, 13, 14, 15, 16), pm to divide sleeve front, k8 (9, 10, 11, 12, 13), pm to divide front/button placket, work in rib to end.

Yoke

Change to larger needles and MC.

Regular raglan rows

Row 1 (WS): Sl 1, work in pattern (knitting the knits and purling the purls) to last st, k1.

Row 2: Sl 1, work to 1 st before raglan marker, *m1, k2, m1, knit to 1 st before next marker; rep from * 3 more times, work in patt to last st, k1—80 (86, 92, 98, 104, 110) sts.

Rep last 2 rows 9 (13, 16, 18, 19, 21) more times, and **at the same time,** after 4th raglan increase row, work buttonhole over next 2 rows, then after every following 12th row as follows:

Buttonhole raglan rows:

WS row: Sl 1, k1, p1, BO 2 sts in rib, then work in pattern to last st, k1.

RS row: Sl 1, increase at raglan markers and work in pattern to buttonhole gap, CO 2, then k1, p1, k1.

When raglan inc are complete, piece should measure 4 (5, 6, 6½, 7, 7½)" (10 [12.5, 15, 16.5, 18, 19]cm) from CO edge, measured along center front—152 (190, 220, 242, 256, 278) sts. End with a RS row.

Divide for Sleeves

Next row (WS): Sl 1, work in pattern to raglan marker, place 31 (40, 47, 52, 55, 60) sleeve sts on waste yarn or holder; CO 4 (4, 6, 6, 8, 8) sts for under arm, p42 (52, 60, 66, 70, 76) back sts, place 31 (40, 47, 52, 55, 60) sleeve sts on waste yarn or holder, CO 4 (4, 6, 6, 8, 8) sts for under arm, work in pattern to last st, k1—98 (118, 138, 150, 162, 174) sts.

Body

Continue in pattern and work rem buttonholes every 12 rows until piece measures approx. 11½ (12, 13, 15, 16½, 18)" (29 [30.5, 33, 38, 42, 45.5] cm) from CO edge and 7 rows past your last buttonhole, ending with a WS row (round measurement up or down a bit as necessary).

Hem

Change to smaller needle and CC.

Row 1: Sl 1, work in pattern to last st, k1.

Row 2–3: Sl 1, [k1 p1], ending with k1.

Row 4: Sl 1, k1, p1, BO 2 sts in rib, then work in pattern to last st, k1.

Row 5: Sl 1, work in pattern to buttonhole gap, CO 2, then k1, p1, k1.

Rows 6–10: Repeat Row 2.

Sl 1 and BO in rib.

Sleeve

Place sleeve sts on larger dpns or long circular for Magic Loop.

Join MC and pick up and k1 st in gap between sleeve sts and under arm CO edge, pick up and k1 st in each st along under arm CO edge, and 1 st in gap between underarm CO edge and sleeve sts—37 (46, 55, 60, 65, 70) sts. Slip last 3 (3, 4, 4, 5, 5) sts from right needle to left needle, pm for beg of rnd at center of under arm. Sl 3 (3, 4, 4, 5, 5) sts back to right needle.

Work in St st and dec at each end of every 7 (8, 8, 9, 9, 10) rnds 7 (8, 8, 8, 9, 9) times as follows: k2tog, knit to last 2 sts, ssk—23 (30, 39, 44, 47, 52) sts. Work even until sleeve measures 8 (10, 11, 12, 13, 15)" (20.5 [25.5, 28, 30.5, 33, 38]cm) from armhole.

Change to smaller needles and CC.

Sizes 1/2 (5/6, 9/10) only: K2tog, knit to end—22 (38, 46) sts.

Sizes 3/4 (7/8, 11/12) only: Knit.

Work 7 rnds in k1, p1 ribbing. BO in rib.

Repeat with other sleeve.

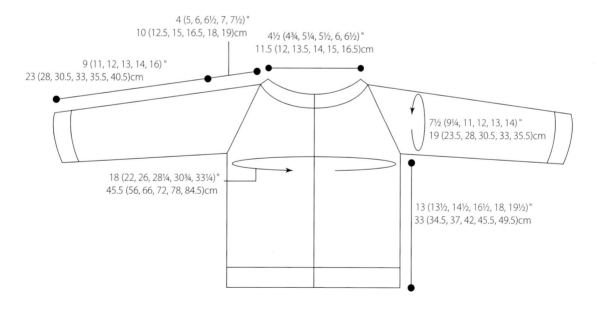

4 (5, 6, 6½, 7, 7½)"
10 (12.5, 15, 16.5, 18, 19)cm

4½ (4¾, 5¼, 5½, 6, 6½)"
11.5 (12, 13.5, 14, 15, 16.5)cm

9 (11, 12, 13, 14, 16)"
23 (28, 30.5, 33, 35.5, 40.5)cm

7½ (9¼, 11, 12, 13, 14)"
19 (23.5, 28, 30.5, 33, 35.5)cm

18 (22, 26, 28¼, 30¾, 33¼)"
45.5 (56, 66, 72, 78, 84.5)cm

13 (13½, 14½, 16½, 18, 19½)"
33 (34.5, 37, 42, 45.5, 49.5)cm

Mockingbirds

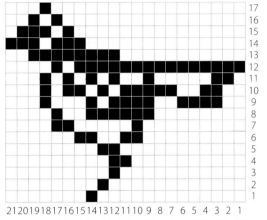

Mockingbird chart for sizes 1/2, 3/4, 5/6.
Mirror chart on opposite sides of sweater.

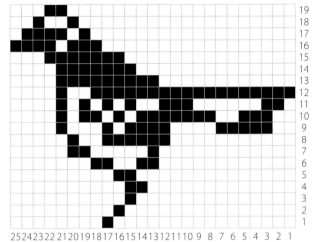

Mockingbird chart for sizes 7/8, 9/10, 11/12.
Mirror chart on opposite sides of sweater.

Place near bottom or breast of sweater. Starting at feet, work one or both charts in duplicate st.

Finishing

Weave in all ends. Block to finished measurements. Sew buttons on left placket opposite buttonholes.

Phoebe Coat

The Catcher in the Rye

S mart and loyal and earnest, Holden's sister Phoebe, with her innocent clarity, is a bright splash in Holden's crummy, disappointing world. Riding on the carousel in her blue coat, reaching for the brass ring, Phoebe captures the simple, joyful hope of youth.

Worked quickly in two strands of Berkshire Bulky and lightly fulled, this coat has vintage charm. The use of clasp closures instead of buttons eliminates the need to fuss with buttonholes and means the same pattern can be used for a boy's coat as well. And the yarn line has an extensive color range, so you could easily make these quick-knitting coats in favorite colors for all the kids on your list.

SIZE
Child 1/2 (3/4, 5/6, 7/8, 9/10, 11/12)

MATERIALS
5 (7, 9, 11, 13) skeins Valley Yarns *Berkshire* (85% wool/15% alpaca, 141yd./129m per 3.5oz./100g). Shown in 30 Blue Ming.

Firmly twisted aran weight single with light luster; develops very fuzzy alpaca halo when fulled.

US 10½ (6.5mm) circulars, 32" (80cm) and 16" (40cm) lengths, *or size needed to obtain gauge*

2 (2, 2, 3, 3, 3) pairs of sew-on coat clasps, loop-and-toggle sets, or heavy-duty hook and eye sets shown in Classic Coat of Arms clasp in Antique Brass finish

Tapestry needle

Stitch markers

GAUGE
12 sts × 17 rows = 4" (10cm) in St st with yarn held doubled, before fulling

Instructions

NOTES: This yarn wet splices very well, so I recommend wet splicing whenever you join a new ball so you'll have fewer ends to weave in at the end.

Schematic measurements **(except length)** are for both knit and fulled garment. Although this seems counter-intuitive, this yarn relaxes when it's soaked. When you wet it, it gets immediately bigger, then after you full it just for a couple minutes, you end up with a size right about the same as your knit size. Full carefully, removing the coat to measure every couple of minutes, as this yarn felts quickly! **This fabric shrinks more vertically than horizontally, so you will lose a bit of length. This pattern has lots** of ease, so if you over-full a bit, the coat will still fit, but it will be much shorter.

This coat is worked from the top down, beginning at the neck.

Raglan Yoke

With shorter circular needle and 2 strands of yarn, CO 29 (34, 34, 39, 39, 42) sts.

Sl 1, k 5 (6, 6, 7, 7, 7), pm, k 5 (6, 6, 7, 7, 7), pm, k 7 (8, 8, 9, 9, 12), pm, k 5 (6, 6, 7, 7, 7), pm, k 6 (7, 7, 8, 8, 8).

Sl 1, k2, purl to last 3 sts, k3.

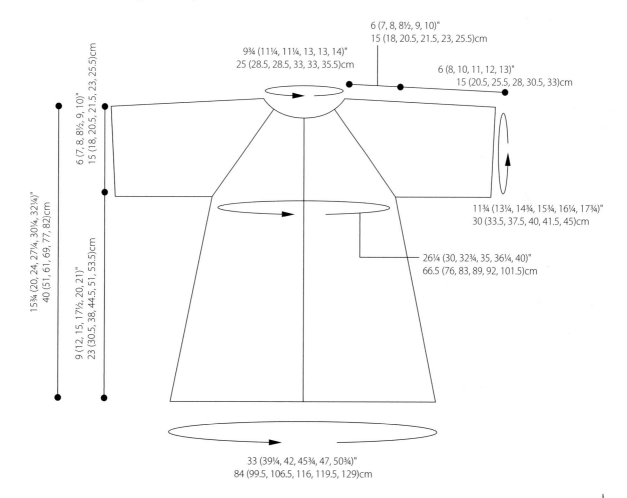

6 (7, 8, 8½, 9, 10)"
15 (18, 20.5, 21.5, 23, 25.5)cm

9¾ (11¼, 11¼, 13, 13, 14)"
25 (28.5, 28.5, 33, 33, 35.5)cm

6 (8, 10, 11, 12, 13)"
15 (20.5, 25.5, 28, 30.5, 33)cm

6 (7, 8, 8½, 9, 10)"
15 (18, 20.5, 21.5, 23, 25.5)cm

15¾ (20, 24, 27¼, 30¼, 32¼)"
40 (51, 61, 69, 77, 82)cm

9 (12, 15, 17½, 20, 21)"
23 (30.5, 38, 44.5, 51, 53.5)cm

11¾ (13¼, 14¾, 15¾, 16¼, 17¾)"
30 (33.5, 37.5, 40, 41.5, 45)cm

26¼ (30, 32¾, 35, 36¼, 40)"
66.5 (76, 83, 89, 92, 101.5)cm

33 (39¼, 42, 45¾, 47, 50¾)"
84 (99.5, 106.5, 116, 119.5, 129)cm

Row 1: Sl 1, [knit to 1 st before marker, m1, k2, m1] 4 times, then knit to end—37 (42, 42, 47, 47, 50) sts.

Row 2: Sl 1, k2, purl to last 3 sts, k3.

Rep Rows 1 and 2 until piece measures 6 (7, 8, 8½, 9, 10)" (15 [18, 20.5, 21.5, 23, 25.5]cm) measured from center back neck—125 (146, 162, 175, 183, 202) sts. Change to longer circular needle when there are too many sts to work comfortably on shorter needle.

Divide for Sleeves

Knit to marker, transfer sleeve sts to waste yarn, CO 3, pm, CO 3, knit across back, transfer sleeve sts to waste yarn, CO 3, pm CO 3, knit to end—79 (90, 98, 105, 109, 120) sts.

Row 1: Sl 1, k2, purl to last 3 sts, k3.

Row 2: Sl 1, knit to end.

Rep Rows 1 and 2 until piece measures 14 (18, 22, 25, 28, 30)" (35.5 [45.5, 56, 63.5, 71, 76]cm) from center back neck, ending with a RS row.

At the same time, inc every 6th (6th, 8th, 8th, 10th, 10th) row 5 (7, 7, 8, 8, 8) times as foll: Sl 1, [knit to 1 st before marker, m1, k2, m1] twice, then knit to end—99 (118, 126, 137, 141, 152) sts.

Hem

Last 3 rows: Sl 1, knit to end.

Next row: Sl 1, then BO all sts.

Sleeves

Transfer sleeve stitches to shorter circular needles.

With RS facing and 2 strands of yarn, beg at center of underarm, pick up and knit 3 along cast-on edge, 1 st in gap between cast-on edge and held sts, knit sleeve sts, pick up and knit 1 st in gap between sts just knit and cast-on edge, then 3 sts along rem cast-on edge—37 (42, 46, 49, 51, 55) sts. Join for working in the rnd, pm for beg of rnd.

Rnd 1: K3, k2tog, knit to last 5 sts, ssk, k3—35 (40, 44, 47, 49, 53) sts.

Work even in St st for 5 (7, 9, 10, 11, 12)" (12.5 [18, 23, 25.5, 28, 30.5]cm), measured from armpit.

Edging

Rnd 1: Purl.

Rnd 2: Sl 1 kwise wyib, knit to end.

Rnd 3: K1, sl 1, purl to end.

Rnd 4: P2, sl 1 wyib, BO all sts kwise.

Collar

With WS facing, longer circular needles and 2 strands of yarn, pick up and knit 28 (33, 33, 38, 38, 41) sts along neck edge.

Row 1: Sl 1, k2, purl to last 3 sts, k3.

Row 2: Sl 1, k2, m1, knit to last 3 sts, m1, k3—30 (35, 35, 40, 40, 43) sts.

Rep last 2 rows 5 (6, 7, 7, 8, 8) more times—40 (47, 49, 54, 56, 59) sts.

Last 3 rows: Sl 1, knit to end.

Next row: Sl 1, then BO all sts.

Pockets

With shorter circular needles and 2 strands of yarn, CO 11 (12, 13, 14, 16, 18) sts.

Row 1: Sl 1, purl to last st, k1.

Row 2: Sl 1, knit to end.

Rep Rows 1 and 2 for a total of 12 (14, 15, 16, 18, 20) rows, then work Row 2 twice and BO on last row, leaving a long tail on one strand to sew on the pocket.

Repeat for other pocket. Weave in all ends except sewing strand.

NOTE: Twirl your needle every several stitches so the yarn's structure remains intact. This yarn has a tendency to untwist as you sew, leaving you with a wispy roving that will just fall apart.

Lay coat out flat and sew pocket so bottom and inside edges run parallel to bottom and center front edges, with top edge falling slightly below waist and top outside corner right at side edge of coat.

Weave in any remaining ends.

Fulling

You can full by hand or in a top-loading washing machine. You need to be vigilant if you're using a machine. The goal isn't to shrink the garment, but to stabilize the fabric and knock out the stretch. It also softens and produces a fantastic, fuzzy halo.

To machine-full, you'll need a top-loading machine that lets you manually control the cycle. Use hot water, a bit of soap, and the normal setting. Agitate for 5 minutes and then turn the cycle to the rinse setting. Allow cold rinse water to refill the machine, agitate for 1 minute only, then turn ahead to the spin cycle.

Block as close to the schematic dimensions as possible, straightening the front, bottom, collar, and cuff edges, and let dry. The length will be a bit shorter than on the schematic.

Clasps

You can sew in the clasps or toggles so that the sides overlap or so that they meet in the center (as in photos). If you're using hooks and eyes, attach so the edges are flush.

Sizes that use two clasps: Sew one clasp at throat and one between armpit and pockets.

Sizes that use three clasps: Sew one clasp at throat, one even with the top of the pockets and one spaced between.

Eppie Bonnet

Silas Marner

Eppie was the golden-haired, cherubic foundling who mended Silas Marner's broken miser's heart. This cheery, unpretentious bonnet is the perfect topper for your own little cherub. The accordioning ribs expand the bonnet's range of sizes, and each size really has the wiggle room to fit the next size up or down.

Though the design is most striking in two colors, it's awfully sweet in a single color as well. And it's also an excellent vehicle for a small amount of a special handspun. Use the handspun as the MC color to showcase the color and texture on both the knit and the purled surfaces.

SIZE
0–9 mos (1–3 years, 4+ years)

MATERIALS
50g each in two different colors of light worsted yarn or 100g in a single color.

Two-tone Bonnet

MC: 1 skein Louet *MerLin* (70% superwash Merino/30% linen, 156 yd./143m per 3.5oz./100g). Shown in 65 Goldenrod.

CC: 1 skein Louet *MerLin*. Shown in 05 Goldilocks.

Smooth worsted with three strands of Merino and two strands of linen. The two skeins are enough for all three sizes if you alternate MC.

Solid Color Bonnet

1 (1, 2) ball(s) Valley Yarns *Sheffield* (70% Merino/15% silk/15% angora, 120 yd./110m per 1.75oz./50g). Shown in 02 Light Blue.

Worsted 4-ply with a silken luster and fuzzy angora halo that increases with wear.

NOTE: Due to larger gauge of this handspun, use the smaller needles for entire bonnet.

MC: 1 skein Spincycle Yarns *Worsted 2-ply* (100% Bluefaced Leicester wool, 120yd./110m per 2.8oz./79g). Shown in Ruination.

Handspun variability with a light luster, dyed before spinning for unique color variation.

CC: 1 ball Valley Yarns *Sheffield* (70% Merino/15% silk/15% angora, 120yd./110m per 1.75oz./50g). Shown in 24 Purple.

Worsted 4-ply with a silken luster and fuzzy angora halo that increases with wear.

US 5 (3.75mm) needles, *or size needed to obtain gauge*

US 3 (3.25mm) straight needles, + 2 dpns for I-cord

GAUGE

21 sts × 26 rows = 4" (10cm) in St st on larger needles

Instructions

Back

With MC, CO 14 (20, 28) sts.

Work 20 (24, 32) rows in St st.

Shape Back

Row 1: K1, ssk, knit to last 3 sts, k2tog, k1—12 (18, 26) sts.

Row 2: Purl.

Repeat last 2 rows twice more—8 (14, 22) sts.

Sides

NOTE: Slip the first stitch and knit the last stitch of every row. The resulting slipped-stitch edge makes picking up stitches along the bottom very easy.

Without turning work, pick up and knit 19 (22, 28) sts along left edge, knit to end, then pick up and knit 19 (22, 28) sts along right edge—46 (58, 78) sts.

Setup Section (3-Row ribs)

MC: Work 3 rows in reverse St st (purl RS rows, knit WS rows).

CC: Work 2 rows in St st (knit RS rows, purl WS rows).

MC: Knit 1 row, then work 3 rows in reverse St st.

5-Row Ribs

CC: Work 2 rows in St st.

MC: Knit 1 row, then work 5 rows in reverse St st.

Rep last 8 rows once more.

7-Row Ribs

CC: Work 2 rows in St st.

MC: Knit 1 row, then work 7 rows in reverse St st.

Rep last 10 rows 0 (1, 2) more time(s).

Edging

CC: Knit 1 row.

Change to smaller needles. Sl 1, k 1, [p2, k2] across row, ending with p2, k2.

Work 4 more rows in rib then BO in pattern.

Bottom

With RS facing, CC, and smaller needles, pick up and knit 56 (62, 90) sts along bottom edge.

TIP: You'll pick up 1 stitch for every 2 rows along the sides (pick up and knit 1 st through each of those slipped-stitch chains) and 1 stitch for each CO stitch along the back.

Continue to slip the first stitch and knit the last stitch of every row.

Sl 1, knit sts along first side; k2tog all sts across the back panel; knit along other side.

Work 2 more rows in reverse St st.

Work 2 rows in St st.

Work 3 rows in reverse St st.

Purl 1 row. Break yarn, leaving sts on needle.

Ties

With CC and dpns, CO 3 sts.

Work 10" (25.5cm) I-cord.

Work applied I-cord edging (see sidebar) along the bottom of bonnet, then work 10" (25.5 cm) of I-cord. BO.

Finishing

MerLin: Soak in hot water, press or spin out excess, then tumble dry medium (the machine-washable blend stretches wet, but snugs back nicely after a tumble dry).

Others: Soak hot, press/spin out excess water, and dry flat.

Applied I-Cord Edging

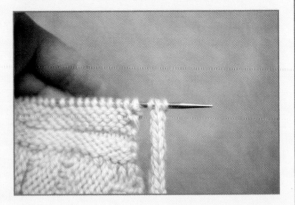

With RS of bonnet facing, slide the I-cord stitches onto needle on right side of bonnet.

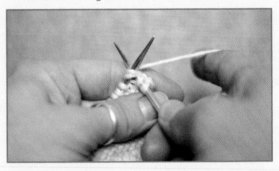

K2, k2tog. You're knitting the first 2 sts of the I-cord, then k2tog with the last I-cord stitch and the first picked up stitch, joining the I-cord to the bottom edge of the bonnet.

Slide the 3 I-cord sts back onto the bonnet needle and rep across all picked up stitches.

Epilogue

Special Techniques

As a rule, I like to knit quickly, keeping the work simple for maximum ease and productivity—and so I can knit in front of the TV or while chatting with friends. So although my general knitting philosophy is "the simpler, the better," I find a few intermediate and advanced techniques really come in handy, and I use them often. The following are a handful of what you might call advanced techniques—but what might just as well be considered shortcuts, for the ultimate savings in construction or assembly.

Kitchener Stitch

The Kitchener stitch is smooth and elegant, magically disappearing into stockinette or garter. And it's easy, after you learn the mantra for both front stitches and back stitches:

- For front stitches: "Knitwise, slip it off; purlwise, leave it on."
- For back stitches: "Purlwise, slip it off; knitwise, leave it on."

The only part that's different is the setup and the ending, where you only use half of the mantra.

Instead of just threading the yarn through each live stitch once, the way you would closing up the top of a hat worked in the round, you work the yarn through each and every stitch twice, from opposite directions (but only once at a time), thereby mimicking the little Vs that form in stockinette. You work stitches in sets of four—two each from each side/needle. Each time, you work only one half of each of the four stitches. When you work the next set of four, you complete one pair (the stitches you slip off) and work the first half of the next pair (the stitches you leave on). That's why the setup stitch is the second half of your mantra ("purlwise, leave it on" for your first front stitch and "knitwise, leave it on" for your first back stitch). You need to set up the rhythm by working only the first half of each of those first two stitches.

If that was as clear as mud, hang in there. It's about to make sense.

NOTE: Before you begin: Both pieces you're seaming must have the same number of live stitches. If one side is off, decrease a stitch somewhere in your last row to make them equal.

Start with your wrong sides together and both needles pointing out the same end. (If you're seaming garter, the last row on both sides should be a WS row.) Hold both needles together in your left hand. I like to separate them with my index finger, leaving the stitches somewhat loose as I go and then adjusting tension at the end.

With a strand about four times the length of the area you're seaming (using the tail off the back needle is often convenient), thread a blunt yarn needle.

Kitchener setup (first stitch on each needle): You're working the *second* beats of your mantra. Remember, your mantra is "[front needle stitches] Knitwise, slip it off; **purlwise, leave it on;** [back needle stitches] purlwise, slip it off; **knitwise, leave it on."** So the setup takes the second beat from each needle—the bolded beats.

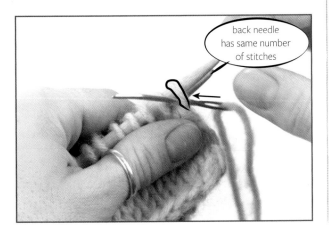

back needle has same number of stitches

"Purlwise, leave it on." Insert the needle through the first *front* stitch purlwise. Leaving the stitch on the needle, pull the yarn through.

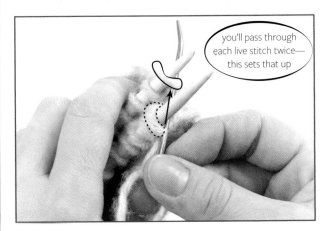

you'll pass through each live stitch twice—this sets that up

"Knitwise, leave it on." Insert the needle through the first *back* stitch knitwise. Leaving the stitch on the needle, pull the yarn through. (The dotted line shows the stitch you worked in the previous step.) Now you're ready to get going on the seam, using your little four-beat mantra.

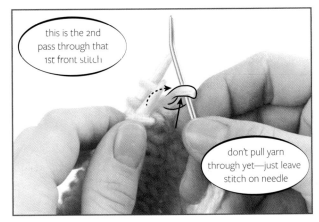

this is the 2nd pass through that 1st front stitch

don't pull yarn through yet—just leave stitch on needle

"Knitwise, slip it off." Insert the yarn needle knitwise through your first front stitch and slip it right off the knitting needle. You're ready to slip this off because this stitch has been passed through twice now: once with the setup and once with this stitch. No stitch slides off the needle until it's been passed through twice.

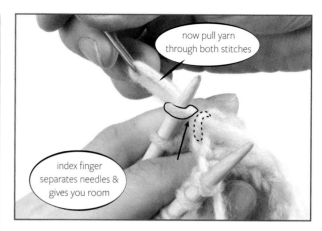

"Purlwise, leave it on." Insert the yarn needle purlwise through your next front stitch. Leaving the stitch on the knitting needle, pull your yarn through, snugging it through both stitches. (The dotted line shows the stitch you slipped off the knitting needle in the previous step.)

"Knitwise, leave it on." Insert the yarn needle knitwise through your next back stitch. Leaving the stitch on the knitting needle, pull your yarn through both stitches. (The dotted line shows the stitch you slipped off in the previous step.)

Then you just repeat the process until you're out of stitches. When you're down to the last two stitches (which will each have been passed through once in the previous step), then you do the *first* beats of your mantra. Again, your mantra is "[front needle] **Knitwise, slip it off;** purlwise, leave it on; [back needle] **purlwise, slip it off;** knitwise, leave it on." So the finish takes the first beat from each needle—the bolded beats.

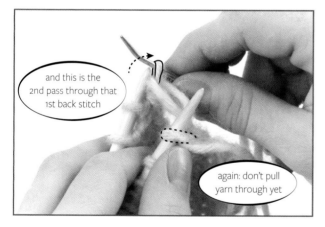

"Purlwise, slip it off." Insert the yarn needle purlwise through your first back stitch and slip it off the knitting needle.

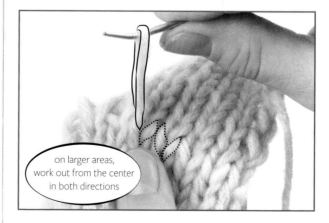

Afterward, you have a single piece of fabric with an irregular "knit" row where they've been joined. Now you adjust the tension to match the rest of the fabric, making the seam invisible. If you've used the live yarn end off one piece, you start at that end and snug up the stitches all the way across. If you've used a separate strand, you can start at the center and work outward. Either way, you might need to make an extra pass or two across to get your tension just right.

seam is soft, flexible and completely invisible

With the tension adjusted, the Kitchener row blends in completely. Voilà!

Short Rows

Short rows involve three steps:

1. The rows themselves, turned part-way across a normal row and worked back the opposite way

2. The wrap, which secures the short rows to the rest of the knitting and prevents a hole

3. Knitting in those wraps so the short rows disappear into the knitting without a trace

When you first started knitting, you probably inadvertently made a few short rows by setting down your knitting mid-row and then picking it up later and working in the wrong direction. You probably discovered your error a few rows later, when you realized that one side of your work was a bit longer than the other, or when you noticed the telltale hole that a short row without a short-row wrap creates.

Short rows are just what they sound like: rows that are worked short of the full row before they're turned and worked in the opposite direction. Short rows enable you to sneak some extra real estate into your

knitting without disrupting the total stitch count of your pattern. The effect is of a couple of partial rows wedged in gently between complete rows.

You can work short rows just on one side (resulting in a wedge shape), or in the center of a piece of knitting, worked in both directions (resulting in a football shape, good for adding extra real estate at the bust of a sweater without making the back longer). Wedges affect the row count on one side (because they're worked all the way to the natural edge), but not the stitch count, whereas footballs (inserted mid row and then worked short of the edge in both directions) change neither the stitch count nor the row count.

In addition to pattern-specific, prescribed shaping, they're a smart and easy way to adjust any pattern when you need a little more room in one area (bust, bottom, pregnant belly) but don't want to go up a size all over.

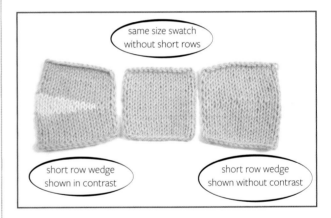

same size swatch without short rows

short row wedge shown in contrast

short row wedge shown without contrast

embedded short rows worked both ways

Short Row Wraps

The short row wrap (which is placed at the end of your short row, before you turn your work) prevents a big gaping hole where you've crammed an extra two rows into the middle of all your knitting.

Any time you turn your knitting, you create an edge. That's just as true in the middle of the row as it would be along the proper side. A keyhole scarf is a good example: Although you're not working short rows, you *are* turning your work mid-row, and it produces an edge, which disrupts the continuous fabric and results in a hole. (In a keyhole scarf, you'd obviously work several rows' worth of edge, but initially the hole results as soon as you turn your work and knit back the other way.)

When you work short rows, you want to wedge in a few extra rows of knitting *without* disrupting the fabric. So to prevent a mid-row edge, and the subsequent hole it makes, you use a special stitch to anchor your short rows to the rest of your knitting: the *short row wrap*. It's basically a little lasso that grabs the stitch after the turn and prevents the normal edge that results when you turn work. The little lasso stands out in a row of stockinette, so you have to knit it in later (see below).

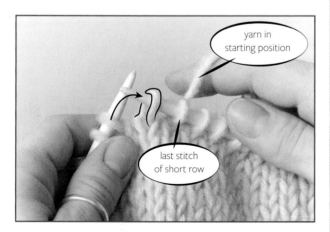

Knit the desired number of short row stitches (pink). Slip the next live stitch purlwise from your left needle to your right needle.

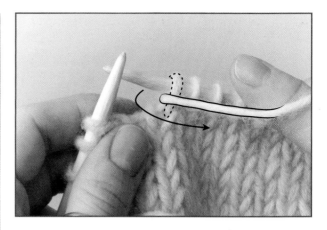

Bring your yarn to the *opposite* side (front, as shown, if you're knitting; back, if you're purling).

Slip that stitch back onto the left needle, where it started. Your yarn is still where you moved it in the previous step (shown front, as you're knitting).

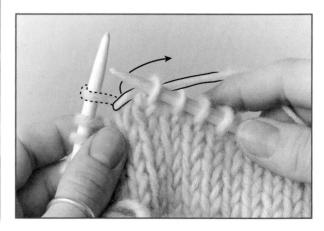

Return your yarn to its original position (back if you're knitting; front if you're purling).

Ta da! See that little purl-like bump that forms a noose around the anchor stitch? That's your wrap. Don't worry; we'll work it right into the knitting in the next step, so it will be totally invisible.

Knitting in Short Row Wraps

Now, if you're working in garter or other textured stitch (for example, linen stitch in the Daisy Cloche project) then you can skip the knitting in because the wrap bumps blend right into the purl bumps, and no one will be the wiser. But if you're using stockinette (for example, in the Elizabeth Bennett top), you need to work those bumps into your knitting. Otherwise, you have an array of what appear to be purls demarking your short row insertions outlines like a little geometry lesson. And you don't want that.

You work the wraps in on the row directly above the wraps, so you only have one chance to get them in. (Don't even think about fixing them a couple rows up—it's a nightmare.) On the knit side, this is all pretty straightforward: You knit in the wraps as you hit them. Working across on the purl side, it's harder because the culprits are on the other side of your work. It's good to hold your work low so you're looking at it from above, which makes it easier to detect those wraps you need to work in. Just because you're working the wrong side doesn't mean the other side of your work disappears. Likewise, half of the wraps—those on the right end of the insert—are harder to work in in the round because you're going against the grain a bit. The sample used here is worked flat. Working round, you see all the wraps on the right side, but the right ones are a little trickier to manipulate. Patience and pointy needles help.

As you approach your wrap, you have two clues: the wrap itself (obvious on the right side; trickier working flat on the wrong side) and the gap on your needle that forms right after the wrapped stitch (or right *before* half of your wrapped stitches if you're approaching the section in the round).

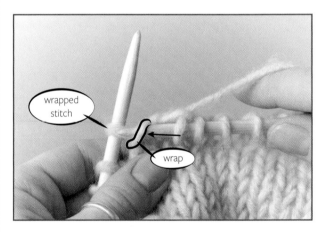

Insert the right needle through the wrap from below, lifting it. (If you're on the wrong/purl side, you still lift the wrap from below, but it is on the backside of your stitch rather than in front.)

Still lifting that wrap, insert your needle through the wrapped stitch as usual. In the sample, I'm on the knit side, so I'm going knitwise. It's almost as if you were about to K2tog. (If you're on the wrong/purl side, you go purlwise, as usual.)

Knit them as one stitch. (Purl them as one stitch from the other side.)

Now you're ready to continue knitting (purling) along your row.

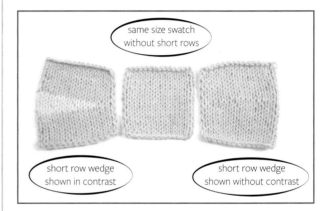

All three swatches have the same stitch and row count, but the two shaped ones have short row wedges (short rows worked in one direction only).

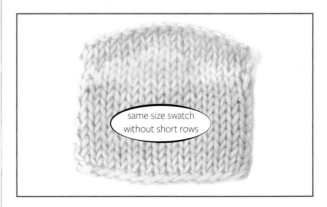

The short rows here are worked in both directions.

Duplicate Stitch

Duplicate Stitch (also known as *Swiss darning*) is just as it sounds: You *duplicate* the existing knit stitches, typically in a contrasting color, to mimic intarsia or Fair Isle without the hassle of carrying two colors and monitoring tension.

Before you begin, if you need extra guidance, you can mark out the perimeters of your chart with safety pins or waste yarn. The original direction of the knitting doesn't matter; just treat each V as one stitch.

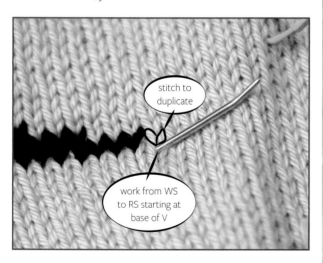

For each stitch you're duplicating, draw your thread from the WS to the RS at the bottom of the V you're working.

. . . then slip the needle under the stitch above…

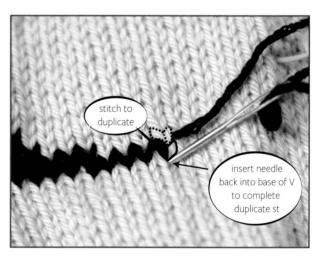

. . . and back down to the bottom of the V to complete the stitch. Repeat for every stitch in the chart, working around the chart in the most comfortable way for you, avoiding long strands in back if possible.

Cabling without a Cable Needle

There are many ways to cable without a cable needle. I think this way is the safest (no loose sts) and easiest, but its limit is about a 4-st cable. Search online for other methods if this one doesn't float your boat.

NOTE: If you would normally hold your cable needle to the front (C2F, etc.), you'll start by working the second half of the cable from the back; if you would normally hold your cable needle to the back (C2B, etc.), you'll start by working the second half of the cable from the front.

C2F

Tilt your work toward you so you can see the back.

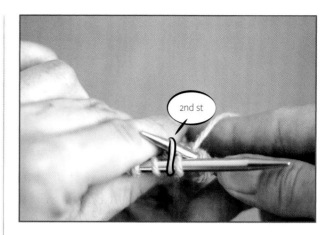

Insert your needle into the 2nd st from back of work and knit it (the original st remains on the left needle, while the st you just knit it on your right needle).

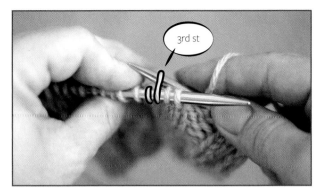

Knit the 1st st (the one you initially skipped) normally, letting the st you knit from behind slip off the needle as well.

Insert your needle into the 3rd st from back of work and knit it (the original st remains on the left needle, while the st you just knit is on your right needle). Repeat with 4th st.

C4F

Tilt your work toward you so you can see the back.

Knit the 1st and 2nd sts (the two you initially skipped) normally, letting the sts you knit from behind slip off the needle as well.

C2B

Insert your needle into the 2nd st and knit it (the original st remains on the left needle, while the st you just knit is on your right needle).

knit 1st st from the front

Knit the 1st st (the one you initially skipped) normally, letting the st you knit in the previous step slip off the needle as well.

C4B

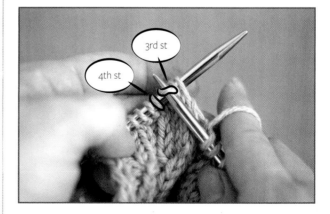

3rd st

4th st

knit 3rd and 4th sts from the front

Insert your needle into the 3rd st and knit it (the original st remains on the left needle, while the st you just knit is on your right needle). Repeat with 4th st.

1st st

2nd st

knit 1st and 2nd st from the front

Knit the 1st and 2nd sts (the two you initially skipped) normally, letting the sts you knit in the previous step slip off the needle as well.

Top-Down Sweater Anatomy

I have a slavish devotion to top-down sweaters for their ease of knitting, seamless styling, and easily customized, try-as-you-go fit. Pretty much every sweater I knit is a seamless, top-down sweater, and they all follow a similar formula, which I've described here.

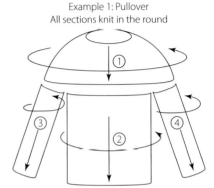

Example 1: Pullover
All sections knit in the round

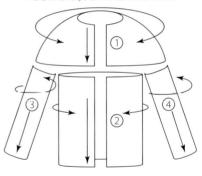

Example 2: Cardigan
1 & 2 knit flat, 3 & 4 knit in the round

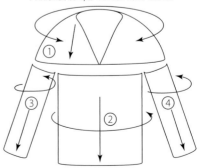

Example 3: V-neck
1 Knit flat to V, 2-4 knit in the round

Cast on at the Collar and Work the Yoke

The pattern dictates whether you work the collar or apply it later, but it all starts at the neck. The yoke, or shoulder portion, consists of a series of increases worked to grow the sweater over the shoulders and down to the armpits. Stockinette raglan sweaters increase at four points (front and back armhole on either side, dividing front, sleeve, back, and other sleeve) every other row, whereas colorwork and other yoke sweaters increase at various points, often more stitches per row with more rows in between increase rows. Generally, the number of increases in stockinette average out to about four per row overall, whereas garter and other squattier stitch patterns have, on average, fewer increases per row. Think of it as increases per inch rather than increases per row, and it all makes sense. (If you're following a pattern, all this math is done for you.)

Divide for Sleeves

Here you transfer the sleeve stitches to waste yarn or spare needles. Cap-sleeved patterns might have you bind off the stitches instead. If you've worked a raglan yoke, all of your math is done already, whereas other yokes divide according to fit. Depending on the desired fit, you might cast on extra stitches over the armpits to expand the sleeves and torso a bit before you continue to work the torso downward, or you might just continue as-is.

Work the Torso

Continue around and around to desired overall length. The torso might or might not include shaping. Finish with desired hem.

Work the Sleeves

Transfer the sleeve stitches back to needles, pick up extra stitches over the armpits if extras were cast on (and/or over the gap, see the "Mind the Gap" section in the Prologue). Work each sleeve in the round, decreasing if called for, to desired length. Finish with desired cuff.

Recommended Reading

Whether you're looking for books to read, historical reference, or just inspiration, get started in print or online with these resources.

General Book Resources

Librivox

Librivox provides access to public-domain recordings of public-domain books. Because they're all volunteer recordings, the quality varies, but there are a lot of gems to listen to online or download to your MP3 player. http://librivox.org (or iTunes)

Project Gutenberg

Project Gutenberg is source for free public domain e-books. www.gutenberg.org

Amazon.com

Amazon.com has thousands of Kindle-formatted public-domain books. If you're a member of Amazon Prime, you can also check out one (non-public domain) Kindle book a month for free. www.amazon.com/Kindle-eBooks

Your Local Library

Duh—it seems obvious, but the library is often terribly underused, so I have to point it out. Now that I live in the sticks, in a rural county with a sadly limited library system, I desperately miss my big public library. If you're lucky enough to have access to a good library, especially one with interlibrary loans (ask your librarian), take advantage! If you haven't been in some time, you'll be thrilled with the selection of audio and e-books, and the ease with which you can search for, reserve, and renew books online.

CraftLit

CraftLit's tagline is "A podcast for Anyone Who Loves Books." Listen while you knit! Visit http://crafting-a-life. com/craftlit, or subscribe through iTunes or Stitcher.

Vintage Pattern Inspiration

Antique Pattern Library

This site has an extensive free collection of PDFs of antique pattern books, which are wonderful for historical knitting or inspiration. www.antiquepatternlibrary.org

Iva Rose Vintage Reproductions

Iva Rose Vintage Reproductions sells high-quality reproductions of rare, out-of-print vintage pattern booklets. It's also a great historical fashion reference. http://ivarose.com

Victoria & Albert Museum

The UK's Victoria and Albert Museum is excellent for general historical fashion inspiration. Search *knitting* for articles, reference, and patterns, including the 1940s pattern selection at www.vam.ac.uk/users/node/1744.

Ravelry

Organize your knitting, commune with other book-loving knitters, and find free patterns and knitspiration at this social networking site for knitters and crocheters. Visit www.ravelry.com to sign up for a free account.

Free Vintage Knitting

Free Vintage Knitting is an archive for out-of-print public domain knitting patterns. The link given here is for women's sweaters, but there are many different categories. http://freevintageknitting.com/women.html

Vintage Knits

Vintage Knits is an online store for old pattern books (originals). It also has a guide to vintage pattern sizes and a database of discontinued yarns (to help you make modern substitutions). http://vintageknits.com

Etsy

You can find old pattern booklets among all the other things you can find at this site. Search for Supplies or Vintage. www.etsy.com

Vintage Knitting Nook

This site provides vintage resources and tips for historic pattern hunting using Trove, Australia's digitized newspaper archive. http://csusap.csu.edu.au/~afahey05

Yarn & Materials Resources

Catherine Bed Socks

Cam Creations (http://silkribbon.com)

Lion Brand (http://lionbrand.com)

Kitty Muff

Blue Sky Alpacas (http://blueskyalpacas.com)

Francie Nolan Tam

Wicked Stitch (http://wickedstitchyarn.com)

Katie Rommely Gaiters

La Mode Buttons (http://blumenthallansing.com/lamode buttons.html)

Mountain Meadow Wool (http://mountainmeadow wool.com)

Wicked Stitch (http://wickedstitchyarn.com)

Meg Mittens

Cam Creations (http://silkribbon.com)

Quince & Co. (http://quinceandco.com)

Jo Mittens

Valley Yarns (www.yarn.com)

Daisy Cloche

Quince & Co. (http://quinceandco.com)

Tess Fingerless Gloves

Louet (http://louet.com)

Emma Shawl

ColourMart (http://colourmart.com)

Elizabeth Bennet Summer Blouse

Blue Sky Alpacas (http://blueskyalpacas.com)

Cam Creations (http://silkribbon.com)

Galadriel Hooded Dress

Araucania (http://araucaniayarns.com)

Frog Tree (http://frogtreeyarns.com)

Meme Shawl

Malabrigo (http://malabrigoyarn.com)

Lucy Honeychurch Shawl

Alpacas of Wildcat Hollow (http://alpacasofwildcat hollow.com)

Jane Eyre Shawl

Cascade (http://cascadeyarns.com)

Lady Brett Ashley Pullover

Shepherd's Wool (http://stonehedgefibermill.com)

Anne Shirley Puff-Sleeve Top

Quince & Co. (http://quinceandco.com)

Ishmael Sweater

Malabrigo (http://malabrigoyarn.com)

Sal Paradise Vest

Valley Yarns (www.yarn.com)

John Thornton Scarf

Blue Sky Alpacas (http://blueskyalpacas.com)

Sydney Carton Cowl

Malabrigo (http://malabrigoyarn.com)

Dorian Gray Fingerless Gloves

Louet (http://louet.com)

Billy Pilgrim Socks

Blue Moon Fiber Arts (www.bluemoonfiberarts.com)

Jojoland (http://jojoland.com)

Vera Videnovich (videnovichfarms.etsy.com)

Oskar Pullover

Valley Yarns (www.yarn.com)

Edmund Crown/Hat

Knit Picks (www.knitpicks.com)

Louet (http://louet.com)

Lyra Hood

Art Club (http://artclubshop.com)

Blue Sky Alpacas (http://blueskyalpacas.com)

Patterns of Time (http://patternsoftime.com or www.amazon.com) for fasteners

Vera Videnovich (videnovichfarms.etsy.com)

Scout Cardigan

Louet (http://louet.com)

Phoebe Coat

Patterns of Time (http://patternsoftime.com or www.amazon.com) for fasteners

Valley Yarns (www.yarn.com)

Eppie Bonnet

Louet (http://louet.com)

Spincycle Yarns (http://spincycleyarns.com)

Valley Yarns (www.yarn.com)

Abbreviations

Abbreviation	Meaning
"	inches
*	repeat instructions after asterisk as directed
. beg	beginning
BO	bind off
CC	contrasting color
circ	circular
cm	centimeter
CN	cable needle
CO	cast on
cont	continue
dec	decrease
dpn(s)	double-pointed needle(s)
est	established
foll	follows
g	grams
inc	increase
incl	including
k	knit
k-b	knit into the row/rnd below
k2tog	knit 2 sts together as 1 (dec)
kfb	knit into front and back loops of 1 st (inc)
kfbf	knit into front, back, and then front again of 1 st (double inc)
kwise	knitwise
LH	left hand
m	marker
m1	make 1 (either direction; inc)
m1l	make 1 left (inc): insert LH needle from front to back under the bar between sts and knit into the back of the lifted bar to twist new st
M1r	make 1 right (inc): insert LH needle from back to front under the bar between sts and knit into the front of the lifter bar to twist new st

Abbreviation	Meaning
MC	main color
oz	ounce
p	purl
p-b	purl into the row/rnd below
p2tog	purl2 sts together as 1
patt	pattern
pm	place marker
psso	pass slipped st over
PU	pick up
rem	remain(ing)
rep	repeat
rev	reverse
RH	right hand
rnd(s)	round(s)
RS	right side
sl	slip (purlwise unless noted)
ssk	slip slip knit (dec): slip 2 sts, one at a time, knitwise, and then knit them together as one
ssp	slip slip purl (dec): slip 2 sts, one at a time, knitwise, return to LH needle, and then purl them together as one
St st	stockinette stitch
st(s)	stitch(es)
T	thrum
tbl	through back loop
tog	together
work even	work in established pattern without increasing/decreasing
WS	wrong side
wyib	with yarn in back
wyif	with yarn in front
yd(s)	yard(s)
yo	yarn over (inc)

Index

About the Author

Nikol Lohr lives and works with her partner, tattoo artist and musician Ron Miller, at The Harveyville Project (http://harveyvilleproject.com), a creative workshop, residence, and retreat housed in two old school buildings on 10 acres in rural Kansas. The Harveyville Project is home to Yarn School, Felt School, Mitten School, Cheese School, Art Club, and Cupcake Ranch.

Nikol is the author of *Naughty Needles: Saucy, Sexy Knits for the Bedroom and Beyond* and is a contributor to *Vampire Knits, Pop Goes Crochet, Alt Fiber,* Knitty, and CRAFT. Her blog is The Thrifty Knitter (thriftyknitter.com). You can also see her designs (including dozens of popular free patterns) at www.ravelry.com/designers/nikol-lohr. If you want to connect online, she is cupcake on ravelry, QueenieVonSugarpants on flickr, and @thriftyknitter on Twitter.

In Nikol's former life, before she relocated to her little paradise in the sticks, she was a web designer in Austin, Texas, and creator of the sem-inal blog Disgruntled Housewife (back from the days when blogs were still called "vanity sites").